CHINA'S BRIGHT FUTURE

THE VIEWS OF A CHINESE THINK-TANK SCHOLAR ON THE WORLD STAGE

WANG WEN

Published by
ACA Publishing Ltd.
University House
11-13 Lower Grosvenor Place,
London SW1W 0EX, UK
Tel: +44 (0)20 7834 7676
Fax: +44 (0)20 7973 0076
E-mail: info@alaincharlesasia.com
Web: www.alaincharlesasia.com

Beijing Office
Tel: +86(0)10 8472 1250
Fax: +86(0)10 5885 0639

Author: Wang Wen
Translator: Teng Jimeng
Editor: David Lammie
Cover art: Daniel Li

Published by ACA Publishing Ltd in association with the People's Publishing House

© 2017, by People's Publishing House, Beijing, China

ALL RIGHTS RESERVED. NO PART OF THIS PUBLICATION MAY BE REPRODUCED IN MATERIAL FORM, BY ANY MEANS, WHETHER GRAPHIC, ELECTRONIC, MECHANICAL OR OTHER, INCLUDING PHOTOCOPYING OR INFORMATION STORAGE, IN WHOLE OR IN PART, AND MAY NOT BE USED TO PREPARE OTHER PUBLICATIONS WITHOUT WRITTEN PERMISSION FROM THE PUBLISHER.

The greatest care has been taken to ensure accuracy but the publisher can accept no responsibility for errors or omissions, or for any liability occasioned by relying on its content.

ISBN: 978-1-910760-46-8

A catalogue record for *China's Bright Future: The Views of a Chinese Think-Tank Scholar on the World Stage* is available from the National Bibliographic Service of the British Library.

CONTENTS

Chapter I
CHINA IS NOT A THREAT, AND IT WON'T COLLAPSE: CHINA IS AN OPPORTUNITY — 1
The collapse of the China collapse theory — 2
Rediscovering China's strength — 9
What will China think when it becomes the world's number one? — 16
Neither inferior, nor complacent: fifteen years after China's accession to the WTO — 22
The West should stop looking at China's changes through the lens of ideology — 26

Chapter II
'REVERSE GLOBALIZATION' IS AN ILLUSION, WHILE GLOBAL GOVERNANCE HAS A FUTURE — 35
The global governance 'revolution' has not yet been accomplished — 36
'Reverse globalization' is an illusion, China is set to lead the new era of globalization — 47
Countries of the world, unite! Let's build a long-term governance mechanism — 52
The TTIP and TPP will go down in history as a mistake — 56
Debunking ten myths about China and the South China Sea — 63
Making the BRICs an engine of the new round of globalization — 68

Chapter III
THE WORLD NEEDS TO REASSESS CHINA'S CONTRIBUTIONS — 81
The world greatly underestimates China's contribution — 82
The US should learn from China in undertaking some political reform — 87
Understanding the Chinese view of climate finance — 93
The China and Africa development paths should not be confined to the Western model — 98

China has the ability to deal with American provocation	104
China taking the lead in the China, US and Russia triangle	113

Chapter IV
THERE'S NO NEED TO OVER-HYPE THE RISK OF THE BELT AND ROAD INITIATIVE — 121

Macro-research on Belt and Road is largely concluded	122
It might be useful to establish 'Belt and Road' studies	128
On the strategic endurance of the Belt and Road initiative after travelling to fifty countries	132
China-US cooperation on the Belt and Road can begin with repairing New York's roads	141
An analysis of the Belt and Road initiative through ten personal stories	147

Chapter V
DON'T BE TOO PESSIMISTIC ABOUT CHINA'S ECONOMY — 157

China is entering its greatest financial era	158
The greatest risk of reform is the fear of risk	162
Why are you so pessimistic about China's economy?	167
Developing 'Made with Chinese Intellect' does not mean giving up labor-intensive manufacturing industry	175
Enhancing ocean awareness and solving China's economic predicament	181

Acknowledgments	190
About the Author	191

I

CHINA IS NOT A THREAT, AND IT WON'T COLLAPSE: CHINA IS AN OPPORTUNITY

THE COLLAPSE OF THE CHINA COLLAPSE THEORY

It would be wrong to assume the future collapse of China's financial and economic institutions. Instead, China is perhaps experiencing the pains of transition and transformation on the eve of a fresh take-off. In fact, the nation is being reborn in much the same way as Chinese folklore describes the Phoenix experiencing Nirvana.

The Chinese government has unlimited responsibilities. For the Communist Party of China (CPC), there are no second chances. It must do a good job in terms of state governance because the country's political culture determines that this is its inescapable responsibility.

Despite the sheer scale of economic activity in China and the significant reforms that have been introduced over the past 40 years, the Chinese government still exercises significant macroeconomic control.

The world is now unable to withstand the collapse of China's economy or its financial meltdown, just as it can't afford a stock market crash on Wall Street.

On July 7, 2014, the Third Sino-German Youth Leaders Conference was held in Lijiang, Yunnan province. Dr. Wang Wen was invited to deliver a keynote speech at the dinner reception.

I'd like to thank the China Institute of Foreign Affairs for giving me the opportunity to address this great audience. I am grateful to the organizers who kindly arranged the meeting to take place in Lijiang, a venue known as the most romantic scenic spot in China, in the hope of taking our minds away from workplace-related stress, worry and occasional pessimism, a state of mind that now prevails among the elite in China, and in Germany too. I say this for a reason and based on a recent survey conducted among industry leaders that shows a pessimistic mood has prevailed among the elite since the 2008 international financial crisis.

Last year, some of my friends working for American thinks tanks told me: "The crisis has become so bad that it is hard to bail out the United States."

A famous German think tank scholar made similar remarks six months ago in a talk he gave at the Chongyang Institute: "The European debt crisis is hard to solve. It's impossible to save Europe." In China, the pessimistic mood also prevails: China is already hopelessly lost. It is natural that the elite class should be more anxious than ordinary people, because they are supposed to be more socially responsible and have more of a sense of crisis. On the other hand, anxiety will lead to misjudgment and inaccurate predictions. In my opinion, at least over the past two decades, the elite projection of China's future development has been utterly wrong, especially when they try to make a case for the so-called 'China collapse theory'.

The first round of speculation that China would collapse took place after 1989, when China's reform and opening-up process was disrupted. With the collapse of the former Soviet Union and the upheavals in Eastern Europe, there was considerable discussion in the West about the possibility of the 'end of history'. Many predicted that China would be the next Communist regime to fall in a tidal wave of democratization. Over the past 20 years, a wave of 'democratization' has swept through Central Asia, West Asia, North Africa, Thailand and Ukraine, but few of these new regimes survived or prospered. Until now, China is the only country to have found its own path of development while resisting Western 'democratization'. So now it can be safely concluded that the 'coming collapse of China' is not actually coming and is therefore utterly wrong.

The second round of speculation about China's coming collapse occurred after 1999 against the backdrop of Chinese banks suffering from high non-performing loans (NPLs), a sluggish labor market due to misguided state-owned enterprise reform that had led to tens of millions of workers being laid off and the Asian financial crisis that caused the Hong Kong financial market crash. In the same year, Gordon Chang's best-selling book *The Coming Collapse of China* was published, in which he predicted the inevitable meltdown of the CPC. This of course failed to materialize and did nothing to hold back China's rapid growth in the 21st century, its GDP rising by more than 10% on average, and the total size of its economy overtaking that of Italy, the UK, France, Germany and Japan, to become the second largest economy within the first decade of the new millennium. Gordon Chang went on to become a laughing stock in the international academic community. By the same token, it is equally wrong to predict an inevitable 'Chinese economic collapse' now.

The third round of speculation about China's collapse began in 2009. It coincided with the unstoppable spread of Web 2.0 technology. Similar to Facebook, Twitter and other microblogs, Renren in China had more than 500m active users. Suddenly, everyone seemed to be empowered to criticize society and the government on the internet. By the end of 2010, with the outbreak of the 'Arab Spring', the London riots of the following summer and the Occupy Movement in the autumn that started in Wall Street and then swept across the globe, some began to predict that Chinese society would enter its own 'winter'. The high-speed train collision that occurred in China in 2011, and public anger over a scandal involving social media celebrity Guo Meimei and her association with the Red Cross Society of China, led to widespread condemnation on Weibo and in the cyberspace in general, and this resulted in huge panic among the general public. The dust has since settled thanks to the reform measures promulgated by the new leadership that emerged from the 18th National Congress of the CPC, which has greatly boosted public confidence in China. Therefore, we should have been able to predict that the so-called coming collapse of China would not materialize.

But the noise made about a China collapse continued. By 2014, the mood of pessimism had run deep, something I called "theorizing China's financial collapse". This pessimistic view is mainly derived from the following concerns: a) danger caused by the current downturn in China's real estate sector; b) the various default risks caused by local debt in China; and c) the economic deterioration caused by a large number of bankruptcy cases. Many people are concerned that China is likely to have a systemic financial crisis. Really? I don't agree.

Then you may ask: how do you explain the current downward pressure on China's economy? My answers are as follows:

First, structural adjustment. In 2008, in order to withstand the international financial crisis, China launched a Rmb4tn economic stimulus policy, resulting in overheated investment. In 2009, the contribution of investment to GDP growth reached 87.6 per cent, far exceeding the financing and recycling capacity of the financial system. The result was that bank loan repayment rates were low, real estate prices rose three-fold and excessive production capacity existed in some industries. All the evidence shows that a dependence on investment-driven growth patterns is unsustainable, and competent authorities must readjust the structure of investment and consumption in economic growth. Therefore, since 2013, China's new economic policy has focused on reducing capacity and de-leveraging, with the immediate result that many prosperous industries, companies and regional economies have experienced unprecedented pressure.

Second, industrial upgrading. Enterprises that are highly energy-consuming and polluting will be gradually phased out in China. At the same time, some low-value-added enterprises will also be eliminated. It is unlikely that China will continue to be a nation that trades 'one hundred million pairs of socks for one Boeing aircraft', nor can it afford to turn Beijing, Shanghai and Guangzhou into smog-affected cities such as London in the 1950s. Besides, industrial upgrading will inevitably cause some old industries, factories and cities to change or even go bankrupt. Therefore, the pressures are clear and present.

Third, deepening reform. I would like to recommend to you the report of the Third Plenary Session of the 18th CPC Party Congress, because it shows that China is currently undergoing the most comprehensive reform in 35 years in areas such as society, the economy, politics, finance, the military and education. Many reform measures are being implemented step by step. In the financial sector, with banking, securities and insurance as its core, new, national-level reform programs are introduced on an almost weekly basis. Reform, for some, means adapting to that pressure.

My German friends, you must be wondering how China can survive this round of economic stress and financial risk. Due to time constraints, I can only briefly address five main points:

First, continued reform. As we all know, China is currently in the middle of an anti-corruption campaign, in which President Xi Jinping and his colleagues hope to build a clean China. The cleaner China becomes, the smoother its reforms will be and the more its economy will grow. In addition, reform in the financial sector will further promote a healthy development of the Chinese capital market.

The second is innovation. In China, companies that are involved in technological innovation will surely perform well, especially internet companies. Many of my entrepreneurial friends are active in internet financing. They make lots of money.

The third is to rely on people's livelihoods. China's current health care reform is operating much more smoothly than Obama's health care reform in the US. In addition, our social security net is gradually improving. In this area, China should learn from Germany. As we all know, China is known for its high savings rate; the people save because they have grave concerns about the costs of health care, education and old age. Thus, as we build a better social security system, Chinese consumers will become more comfortable with spending their money. Therefore, the economy will improve.

Fourth, new urbanization. China is building several city clusters, including the Beijing-Tianjin-Hebei cluster and the Yangtze River Economic Belt, each of which has 100m consumers. In addition, nearly 300m people will migrate from the rural countryside to urban areas in the next 10 years. There is great economic growth potential here.

The fifth is opening up. China and its neighboring countries will sign more free trade zone agreements. What is more noteworthy is that China will embark on its Belt and Road project that will incorporate central and Western Europe, with Germany and other countries as its terminus. If completed, it will change the lives of 3bn people in Eurasia.

My conclusion is that it would be wrong to assume the collapse of China's financial and economic institutions. Rather, China is perhaps experiencing the pains of transition and transformation on the eve of its fresh take-off. In fact, the nation is being reborn in much the same way as the Phoenix experiences Nirvana, according to Chinese folklore.

I would like to evoke the following three areas of logic when it comes to thinking about China.

The first one is bottom line logic. The Chinese government is a government with unlimited responsibility, if you allow me to use the term. European and American governments have only limited liability in the sense that, if the economy fails to perform well enough, they can just step down, no big deal. They can always come back in a few years. However, for the CPC, there is no second chance to do a good job of governing the country. It must be done well because the CPC is duty-bound. This is determined by China's political culture.

The second is the logic of politics. Despite the sheer scale of economic activity in China and the significant reforms that have been introduced over the past 40 years, the Chinese government still exercises significant macroeconomic control.

The third is of global politics. The world is now unable to withstand the collapse of China's economy or its financial meltdown, just as it can't afford a stock market crash on Wall Street.

So here, blessed by the beauty of the city of Lijiang, let's think about the bright future of China's ever-growing development, let's work together to find common opportunities for our two countries and play the role of young people in our two countries.

I'm sure everyone's hungry, so I will conclude shortly. Before doing so, however, I want to make three wishes. I hope everyone has a fond and memorable experience in Lijiang. Second, today is July 7. Seventy-seven years ago, Japan invaded China, causing more than 30m Chinese casualties, but their government has yet to face up to history. I hope that

Japan will learn from Germany in its attitude to its wartime past. Finally, I hope Germany beats Brazil at tomorrow's World Cup semi-final and advances to the final, before going on to hopefully win the World Cup, because the German team has been my favorite for the past 20 years.

REDISCOVERING CHINA'S STRENGTH

―――

Western thoughts, theories and policy recommendations introduced into China over the past thirty years have often proved quite problematic. In contrast, homegrown Chinese political and economic policies have been quite successful. Perhaps the Chinese people will need a fourth round of 'opening up, eyes wide open style' in order to comprehensively compare the differences between China and the rest of the world. Therefore, it becomes a historic mission to rediscover China's strengths and possible weaknesses. It will take the efforts of our generation and future generations, or an even longer period of time, to accomplish this mission.

On the afternoon of December 9, 2014, the Research Center for China Development Model was officially launched at Fudan University. This is the world's first research center devoted to the study of the China model. Dr. Wang Wen was invited as a keynote speaker to address the opening conference.

THANK YOU, PROFESSOR WANG SHAOGUANG, FOR YOUR KIND introduction. First of all, I would like to congratulate Professor Zhang Weiwei on inaugurating this center. I am very honored to be one of those involved in editing his first batch of articles, which began in 2007 and 2008. My heart was full of pride for I was a witness when these ideas about the rise of China were first conceived. Professor Zhang was generous enough to thank me in the postscripts of his seminal works, *China Shocks the World* and *China Touches the World,* which have sold millions of copies in China. I'd also like to take this opportunity to thank you in return. [Audience laughs]

Professor Zhang Weiwei is a key intellectual figure in theorizing the rise of China over the past decades. In fact, this is the first research center in China set up in the wake of the country's rise whose impact has been felt widely around the world. It is indeed a timely event. This is the first point I would like to make.

I'd like to make the second point in the form of a question: who are the masterminds, specifically scholars or thinkers, behind such a great process, namely, the trend towards the China-rise narrative? At some point around 2008, there was a craze to study the China model in the Chinese intellectual community. Or, let me put it this way: why is it Zhang Weiwei? Why does it have to be Professor Zhang and his congenial spirits who are widely identified as the flagship thinkers in this group? My personal research findings indicate that the process is actually driven by three types of scholars.

The first type includes foreign friends such as Professor Robert Lawrence Kuhn and Professor Martin Jacques who are known for being critical of European and American politics. They have a special feeling for and objective understanding of China. They demonstrate a rare courage to examine China in different ways. The second batch of scholars are those who used to work or study abroad, or those who have acquired their doctoral degrees and therefore have developed a deep understanding of the West. They are well versed in Western political theories, yet they think beyond the constraints of Western perspectives. There are many of you in this audience, for example Wang Shaoguang, Pan Wei, Shi Zhengfu and other professors, most of whom have been in the US for more than 10 years. The third and last group of scholars are those who often travel overseas, whose scholarship is acquired through walking on their feet – doing field trips. Instead of adhering to textbook theories, they choose to seek truth from facts. Professor Fang Ning, who is invited to grace the function here today, is one of the most outstanding scholars of this group. Over the past few years, he has been traveling extensively in East Asia, including to five countries and a region. Almost single-handedly, he rediscovered a model of political power transfer unique to countries in East Asia, which was widely acclaimed as a major breakthrough in China's comparative political studies.

In general, this group of scholars rediscovered the Chinese development model and tried to elaborate on the root cause of the advantages of the Chinese system. Admittedly, the discovery is based on their profound knowledge of the international affairs of the state, as well as their full confidence in China's development through a thorough comparative study of nations of the world.

China's confidence has been acquired after a very arduous process. It has taken around two hundred years. Since 1840, China has repeatedly undergone the process of 'opening to the outside world – introducing advantages – restoring confidence – frustration – opening up again'. After the first round of opening up in 1840 characterized by the intellectual traffic of ideas from the West to China, Western advanced technology was introduced. At that time, due attention was directed to 'looking at the world with eyes wide open' and 'learning skills from the barbarians' and so on. So the focus was mostly on science and technology, the means of industrial production. National confidence was briefly restored during reform-oriented movements such as 'the Self-strengthening Movement' and 'the Reform Movement of 1898'. The self-deceitfully proud Boxers were an extreme example. But tragic defeat in the First Sino-Japanese War of 1895 resulted in a major setback for China's plan to acquire superiority through introducing Western technology. Once again, China was forced back on track to search for the force behind its rejuvenation.

The second round of opening up began around 1911-19. Seminal events included the overthrow of the Qing dynasty followed by the founding of a republic. Then, the salvoes of the Russian October Revolution in 1917 sent Marxism to China, as the old saying goes. What made this part of the experience unique was that China introduced a political theory with an emphasis on the theory of democracy and classic Marxist doctrine. But the Kuomintang government's defeat and the early setbacks suffered by the People's Republic of China (PRC) once again proved that it is not feasible to promote them in a dogmatic way, be it democratic theory or Marxist doctrine. Instead, what seems to work in localizing these theories in China is to involve the people and society at large as part of building national strength.

The reform and opening up of 1978. This was the third round of opening to the outside world in modern China, and the core of this round was the introduction of economic theory centered on the free market doctrine. This openness coincided and resonated with the early expectations of China's 'marketization and democratization' by Europe and the United States. So, from the 'China-US honeymoon period' in the 1980s, to the 'engagement' and 'hedge off' policy of the US towards China in the 1990s, to Western support for Beijing's bid to host the Olympic Games and China's accession to the WTO by the end of 2000, and cooperation with America's war on terror, all of which helped China believe that it had truly integrated itself into the world. By the same token, the West thought it was also time to democratize China. However, around 2008, there was a sharp turn in the state of affairs. James Mann, author of *The China Fantasy* and a major voice among Western liberals, began to raise the question: "Can an economically successful China become a democratic country?" At that time, the US Senate held two hearings on the issue, and the conclusion was more tilted towards 'nay'. As a result, when Beijing hosted the Summer Olympic Games, there was an unprecedented resistance from Europe and the United States. China may have awoken again but it still failed to win respect of the other great nations, like Sister Xianglin, the tragic female character in Lu Xun's *New Year's Sacrifice*, who had paid for admission but still could not enter the hall of her ancestors. In sharp contrast to the consequences of the financial crises in Europe and America, the success of the Beijing Olympic Games and the Shanghai Expo has greatly boosted China's self-confidence in formulating its own theory and choosing its own path of development.

Therefore, the three reasons that led to the 'political thought craze' to rediscover China's strength before and after 2008 can be summed up as follows. First, it was a natural response to the historical setbacks over the previous century. The second was a self-reflexive move in response to repression that came from every spectrum of the West. Third, a summary by a group of pioneer thinkers who had a true understanding of the strengths and weaknesses of Western countries.

Now, in retrospect, the body of European and American ideological and theoretical policies that were conveyed from the West to China over the past thirty years has often been very problematic. One of these is the housing marketization policy. Although it has helped increase the wealth of a considerable number of people, marketization of housing has become a major source of social problems and unrest. Another is the car culture. Since 2000, Chinese society has been tangled up in a debate over whether or not to build an automobile society. In just a few years, China has become the largest dumping ground for automobiles in the world. This has led to a range of problems including the energy crisis, environmental degradation and rising levels of respiratory and other diseases.

By contrast, homegrown political and economic policies have been quite successful. My hometown Yiwu in Zhejiang province is a case in point. Here, farmers would initially get involved in business by trading 'chicken feathers for sugar', for example, before the town evolved into the world's largest commodity distribution center. The transformation of cities such as Yiwu has enabled China to surpass the US in foreign trade volume and become the largest trading nation in the world. Also, the CPC, by pooling the collective wisdom of the Chinese people, implemented the household contract responsibility system, as well as the most recent land transfer policies put forward in the decision of the Third Plenary Session of the 18th CPC Congress. From this point of view, I am afraid that the Chinese need to have a fourth round of its campaign to 'see the world with eyes wide open', with the purpose of providing a comprehensive comparison of the differences between China and the world. The idea is to identify the real gap so that we, as China, can continue to evolve and improve. In particular, we must never copy existing foreign models.

I think this round of 'seeing the world with eyes wide open' also requires a lot of hard work because it is bound to be accompanied by a most difficult process characterized by a major shift from a 'deficit' to a 'surplus' in the intellectual exchange of ideas from China to the West. Early on, the first shift from deficit to surplus began with small commodities and light industrial products, followed by heavy industrial products manufactured by the likes of Sany and high-tech items by Huawei and others. Gradually, it has taken the form of films and television programs, Confucius Institutes and other cultural products. The last trade deficit occurs in the area of intellectual thought. Products in this area are in short supply because almost all the excellent social science books that sell better are translated books, normally 10 times more than books written by local scholars. I'm currently studying finance, and I have found that the same trend is happening in books on finance. Fortunately, a large number of Chinese financial experts have come to realize that what has prevailed in Wall Street should not be all allowed to apply in China. That is why ideas emerge such as 'finance must be pressed to service the real economy' as well as many others that run counter to the mainstream arguments prevailing in the American financial community.

Speaking against this general background, Professor Zhang Weiwei and many distinguished scholars here in this room are burdened with a major mission. Furthermore, rediscovering China, namely rediscovering its strengths and weaknesses, will remain a great historic mission, which may take the efforts of one or two generations or perhaps even longer to accomplish.

The third is a suggestion. With the establishment of the current research center, two priorities stand out. In addition to the in-depth study of China's development model, two things should be highlighted at this point: first, mass dissemination so that the general public is better informed about the advantages and disadvantages of China's development model. For me, there is an element of reverse racism in current Chinese public opinion. By that I am not saying that it is bad for Chinese people to conduct some occasional self-criticism, but if it is excessive, it will lead to nothing but an unwanted sense of inferiority. A typical case in point was the incident that occurred in Shanghai the day before yesterday when an old woman was hit by a foreigner's car. At the beginning, national public opinion overwhelmingly blamed the lady for falsely accusing the foreigner. If it were not for the video footage, there would be no way for the old lady to defend herself. Similar events emerge on an almost daily basis. Once an event like this occurs, it is the Chinese, sadly, who are to blame. Values come first in judging and resolving disputes. A general lack of confidence on the part of the general public leads to misjudgment, and therefore the trend of excessive self-criticism without proper judgment should be reversed. This, I suggest, should be also an important responsibility of the Research Center for China Development Model at Fudan University.

The second is intergenerational experience-sharing. That is the local advantage of China in terms of passing the wisdom and thought of the masters down to younger generations of scholars. Young people are very important. Sometimes I find that it is those young people who receive higher education who tend to look down on the Chinese themselves, their parents and the local ways of doing things. Most of them will take senseless pride in knowing just a few words of Pidgin English or academic jargon. It is not that the West does not have any merits, nor is it bad to criticize China. What I mean is that we are Chinese – why bother to be 'bananas', or yellow in skin color but white at heart? Therefore, the question of how to educate, guide and train China's younger generation so that they become more confident, more objective and more rational when examining the differences and gaps between China and the world, is also a great responsibility of the Research Center for China Development Model. Of course, as a member of the new generation of scholars, I am also obliged to commit myself to this work. From the perspective of Chongyang Institute for Financial Research, Renmin University of China, I will continue to contribute my bit to a China in transition and transformation, yet with a very promising future ahead of us. So, I do not agree with Mr. Martin Jacques in saying that "China has been successful". I think that, at most, China is only 'halfway down the road to success'. Or to quote Dr. Sun Yat-sen's adage: "The revolution is still unfinished, Comrades. We still need to work hard." Perhaps we will need to work hard and overtime.

WHAT WILL CHINA THINK WHEN IT BECOMES THE WORLD'S NUMBER ONE?

As it gradually assumes the mantle of having the world's largest economy, China hopes to become a responsible power and the first in world history to achieve ascendancy without fighting a war but instead through implementing the Belt and Road initiative.

On November 24, 2016, the Third China Forum on the Belt and Road Initiative: New Opportunities and New Challenges was held in Austria's second largest city, Graz. Dr. Wang Wen was invited as the opening keynote speaker to address the topic of 'Global transformation and progress in China's Belt and Road initiative'. As a speaker, he was jointly selected by the Chinese and European organizers. This text is based on his original English transcript.

First off, I'd like to thank the organizers for the invitation. But my special thanks go to Ambassador Li Xiaosi and President Chen Wanjie for their hard work to make this forum possible, and for giving me the opportunity to visit the Austrian city of Graz. In this classy and beautiful city, I feel like being baptized in the aura and antiquity of European and Austrian cultures and history. In this regard, China has much to learn from Europe in general and Austria in particular.

On the other hand, I also feel a bit disappointed. I wanted to visit Mr. Danilo Turk, former president of Slovenia. He is a senior research fellow at Chongyang Institute for Financial Research, Renmin University of China. He is now based in Ljubljana, the capital of Slovenia, which is about 200km from Graz, similar to the distance from Beijing to Tianjin, the two largest cities in the north of China. It is perfectly normal now for a person who lives and works in Beijing to spend 34 minutes on a high-speed train ride to Tianjin for a dinner appointment, and then head back home to Beijing. But the journey from Graz to Ljubljana is said to take more than three hours; I am afraid I will not be able to fulfill my wish to visit Mr. Turk with so many hours to be spent on the road.

Since 1980, having maintained an average growth rate of about 10 per cent, China has leapfrogged from being an underdeveloped country into the world's second largest economy. One major reason identified by most scholars around the world to explain China's rise to become the world's leading economy in the next 10 years or so, is its infrastructure construction. China is connected through expressways at county-level and high-speed railways at city level. This transportation system allows materials, personnel, technology and products to flow quickly in the world's largest market of 1.3bn people. The interconnection has made it possible for the Chinese economy to increase by 100-fold over the past 30 years.

If I am allowed to share one thing central to China's economic rise, it is the interconnectivity through infrastructure building. In Chinese we say: "To get rich, build roads first." China's economic development proves that interconnectivity is the cornerstone of social mobility and economic expansion. In addition to being an important indicator of a nation's strength, instead of its military power, interconnectivity can also be the road to human salvation. Why do I say that? Well, I must start with the global transformation! In fact, I have summed up six general points:

First, the Asia-Pacific region being the global center. The Asia-Pacific has become the most dynamic region in the global economy. China, in particular, is now the second largest economy in the world and the largest exporter. In the next five to eight years, it will become the world's largest importer, the largest overseas investor, the largest consumer market and the largest economy. In this case, China must provide public goods to the world, which is why I am about to discuss the Belt and Road initiative.

Second, international interaction through networking. We rely on networks, not just human networks, but also traffic networks. We also rely on the information, mobile and payment networks. In many Chinese cities, all payments and purchases can be made with a single mobile phone. Business transactions have been greatly accelerated and many new economic values have been generated. And the Belt and Road initiative I would like to elaborate on here is a network between countries and their peoples.

Third, the securitization of social assets. The so-called 'ratio of financial assets to GDP' in developed countries is generally between 4.5 and 5, that is, financial assets are four-to-five times that of GDP. Since a great deal of wealth has been concentrated in financial markets, it is the responsibility of the financial authorities of every big power to maintain and increase the values of wealth and work out how to make our property more stable. The Belt and Road initiative provides an opportunity for financial market interconnectivity to achieve global financial stability.

Fourth, competition among interest groups in the public domain. In the original market, the interest composition of the various stakeholders is almost solidified, while the structure of interest has become ossified. For an interconnected global economy to happen, we must rely on larger markets, and more potential markets, to achieve this. Now, apart from markets in developed countries and the Asia-Pacific region, there are also new markets in Asia and Europe, and African countries, as well as countries in South Asia and the Middle East. Furthermore, there are more 'public domains', such as the internet, the North and South Poles, space, the oceans. The Belt and Road initiative aims to make these public domains new markets for economic growth through connectivity.

Fifth, continued economic growth as a new normal. Without substantial technological innovation, plus the fact that some countries are moving towards trade protectionism, it will be a great challenge for the global economy to recover to the level before the 2008 financial crisis. The Belt and Road initiative intends to restore global economic growth momentum through connectivity and maintain sustainable growth among those economies currently growing at moderate and high rates.

Sixth, the fragmentation of value-orientations. Worldwide, there is an unprecedented skepticism about the democratic model and the Washington Consensus. Countries around the world aspire to charter new courses for change. China is the only country that continues to press ahead with its own reform programs. And the rationale behind China's Belt and Road initiative is to share its reform experience with the world and help the world develop further.

So what exactly is the Belt and Road initiative? This is a brief chronology of events. In September 2013, Chinese President Xi Jinping made the proposal during his state visit to Kazakhstan, officially known as 'Building the Silk Road Economic Belt' initiative. In October that same year, when visiting Indonesia, he initiated the 'construction' of the Twenty-First Century Maritime Silk Road. Hence, the Belt and Road initiative. On March 28, 2015, three Chinese ministries and commissions jointly published the only article on the Belt and Road initiative, entitled 'Building Belt and Road: Vision and Action'. The key word is 'interconnectivity'. It includes the 'five links', which are:

Policy communication. China hopes that policy communication between countries can be smoother.

Infrastructure connectivity. China wants to help the world build more airports, harbors, roads, railways and tunnels, as we have done in China for the past 30 years.

Trade connectivity. China hopes to accelerate trade among nations, allowing consumers across the world to enjoy better quality products.

Financial connectivity. China hopes to facilitate financial transactions, clearing and other financial cooperative projects.

People-to-people connectivity. China hopes that there will be more exchanges among people and better understanding of the people through direct contact.

These ideas will have been developed by the time China becomes the world's leading economic power. Over the past three years, the Belt and Road initiative has made significant progress, exceeding the expectations of the general public in China.

Policy connectivity

- Bilateral cooperation: Until now, 56 national or regional organizations have signed the 'Joint Declaration of the Belt and Road Initiative' with the PRC government.
- Multilateral cooperation: 16 international multilateral cooperation mechanisms have been designed to carry out Belt and Road projects.
- Exchange visits by high-level government officials: high-level visits by heads of state involving China and 40-plus countries.
- Strategic docking: the development strategies of 10-plus regions or countries are integrated with Belt and Road.

Infrastructure connectivity

- Standard docking: 10 directions and 13 key areas
- Traffic links: 39 railway lines for China-Europe freight trains
- Energy connectivity: 40 major energy projects, involving 19 countries
- Free flow of information: 55 countries deploy 4G telecoms technology TD-LTE commercial networks.

Unimpeded trade

- Trade facilitation: 22 countries and regions have signed free trade agreements with China.

- Investment facilitation: 104 countries have signed bilateral investment agreements with China.
- Cooperation platform: China has established economic and trade cooperation zones with 18 countries.

Finance

- Trade settlement: the value of cross-border renminbi settlement has reached Rmb2.63tn under current account of Belt and Road countries.
- Financing through development: China accounts for 70 per cent of the total investment in government-dominated development projects

Cultural exchange

- Cooperation in culture and education: China's government offers 10,000 Belt and Road scholarships each year.
- Health care: more than 23,000 Chinese doctors on foreign aid programs are working in 67 countries around the world.
- Cooperation in science and technology: 56 Belt and Road countries have signed a memorandum of understanding on cooperation in science and technology with China.
- I conclude that, as China gradually becomes the world's new superpower, it is becoming a responsible big country through the pursuit of the Belt and Road initiative. It is also China's hope that it will become the first country in the history of the world to rise without fighting a war.

Finally, please support China, for this new global power wants to contribute to the world. Please engage China, for China wants to learn from the world. Please invest in China, which is a world-renowned emerging economy.

It happens that today is Thanksgiving Day.

Thank you, Austria, for your support over the years. Thank you for your attention.

NEITHER INFERIOR, NOR COMPLACENT: FIFTEEN YEARS AFTER CHINA'S ACCESSION TO THE WTO

Fifteen years after its accession to the World Trade Organization, China should feel neither humbled nor complacent. The country cannot take the same path as the UK or the US, and it will never seek hegemony. Yet the key is that China's rise may not be easy by changing global rules or through bilateral and multilateral cooperation, given the fact that its rise will not be achieved through war. However, I do believe that time is still on its side.

On December 13, 2016, the 15th Annual Conference on the WTO and China was held at the University of International Business and Economics in Beijing. Dr. Wang Wen was invited to deliver a keynote speech at the conference.

IF THE GROWTH OF A BIG POWER IS COMPARED TO THAT OF A PERSON, China's growth from 2001 to 2015 represents that key period of transition from teenager to adult. I think it makes sense if I compare China's reform and opening up, which began in 1978, and its rise as a modern and a major power in the world to the key period of human growth from the age of 22 to 37. Likewise, I consider today's talk as a rewarding experience as I return as a college graduate to share with you my worldview and outlook on life.

Two changes can be identified:

The first 15 years, from a follower of the rules to a reformer and leader of the rule-making process. In 2001, after 15 years and five months of arduous negotiations, China became fully integrated with global rule-based governance and practices. It also conducted difficult negotiations with competent organizations over agreements such as The Agreement on Trade Facilitation and The Agreement on Information Technology. According to official data, approximately 2,400 national legal and administrative regulations were repealed, modified or drafted in order to comply fully with the global rules and regulations. About 200,000 local laws and regulations were revised accordingly. By complying with international rules, China is on a fast lane to becoming a country with ruled-based governance.

In terms of internationalization, China has launched free trade zone trials in Shanghai, Guangdong, Tianjin, Fujian, Liaoning, Zhejiang, Henan, Hubei, Chongqing, Sichuan and Shaanxi. It also implements a free trade zone strategy in the Asia-Pacific region.

The process of marketization has been accelerated. Since July 1, 2004, China has fulfilled its commitment to liberalize its foreign trade management rights six months ahead of schedule. The registration and filing system has replaced the examination and approval system of foreign trade rights, ending a practice that had been in place for 50 years. On January 1, 2005, China abolished the quota license system for imported cars and implemented automatic import license management for auto products. On July 1, 2006, China's tariffs for imported autos completed its final reduction since accession to the WTO, down from 28 per cent to 25 per cent. The tariff rate on imported auto parts was also reduced, to 10 per cent. In doing so, China had fulfilled its commitment to reduce taxes on autos and auto components upon joining the WTO. In addition, since January 1, China brought an end to the foreign-funded enterprises' tax rate differentiation, a practice that had prevailed in China for almost 20 years.

However, with its comprehensive strength dramatically improved and well positioned to exert more power in trade rule-making, China began to play a role in formulating and guiding the development of new rules using the Belt and Road initiative as a platform. Here are some examples: the G20 Global Trade Growth Strategy, adopted at the 2016 G20 Summit as the new approach to trade; the world's first framework of multilateral investment rules, the Guiding Principles for the G20 Global Investment, as the new investment principle; and the New Technical Standards for Global Railroad Crossing developed with China railway's standards as the core.

The second change occurred 15 years after China's accession to the WTO, when its role switched from being a beneficiary of globalization to a contributor to globalization. Over the past 15 years, China has been transformed from a nation with a relatively weak trade and economy to the world's second largest economy, the largest trading nation, the largest recipient of inward foreign investment and the second largest outward investor, creating tens of millions of jobs across the world.

In the next five to 10 years, China will become, among other things, the largest economy and the largest importing market in the world, contributing as much as 40 per cent of global economic growth, thus becoming the chief contributor to global trade, and economic and investment growth. More important, the Belt and Road initiative has become a stabilizer and accelerator of the global economy.

In addition, there are two significant changes that have yet to happen.

First, skepticism and suspicion of China in the West has not changed. Changes are occurring in developing countries, but it will take a while for the West to come to terms with China. For example, until now the EU has refused to grant market economy status to China, which means that China remains the biggest economy in the world with the largest number of anti-dumping and countervailing investigations. In 2015, 17 countries and regions initiated 75 anti-dumping and countervailing investigations against China.

Second, the Chinese are still not adapting to international rules and regulations and global practices. Prior to 2008, the growth of global trade was about 1.8 times the growth rate of the world economy. But it has now been five consecutive years that the world economy has been growing at a slower rate. To make things worse, international competition will become even more brutal in some respects. With China still not very adaptable to international planning, a growing need has arisen for the country to familiarize itself better with international practice, and to train more professionals who are adaptable to international competition and more receptive to knowledge and the rules of the game.

I conclude that, having been in the WTO for 15 years, we should feel neither inferior, nor complacent. That said, it is quite remarkable for the same political party, and the same people, to have achieved so much over the past 30 years. However, it is quite clear that, on the one hand, the road is getting narrower and narrower in order to achieve industrial upgrading by simply relying on low labor cost advantages to develop processing trade; while on the other hand, a Western-style rise to dominance may not work in the current world. Britain created an empire on which the sun never set, having fought three major wars with France, a naval war with Spain and a war against the Russians in the Crimea. The US became the world's largest economy in the 1890s, yet it took another 50 years for it to become a global leader. China will not follow the same path as either the UK or the US. Nor will China seek hegemony by means of war. Even so, China's rise is unlikely to be easy through changing global rules or through bilateral and multilateral cooperation. However, I do believe that time is still on China's side.

THE WEST SHOULD STOP LOOKING AT CHINA'S CHANGES THROUGH THE LENS OF IDEOLOGY

In China, the media is a major contributor to national development, social stability and economic reform. It also subjects itself to state governance, acting out the role of gatekeeper, committed to preventing the general public from being overwhelmed with information that may cause political turmoil. Furthermore, Chinese media ensure the exchange of information that is necessary for 1.4bn people to interact with one another so that public opinion can be expressed, but not in an extremist way that can lead to political disorder and social unrest. In fact, this is actually the third way for media to develop in China, a path of incrementalism to take for Chinese media and political democratization.

With the rapid development of new media, traditional media outlets face a crisis. The rise of new media has also posed new challenges to political governance. But Western media continue to deal with China with double standards, maintaining that China's censorship system will unlikely be overturned even with the arrival of new media. To what extent does the Western media misunderstand and misrepresent China? What can be done to defuse misunderstandings by the creation of a new type of think tank that co-exists with the new media? On August 18, 2015, Dr. Wang Wen delivered a keynote speech at the Beijing Alumni Association of the London School of Economics and Political Science.

THANK YOU VERY MUCH FOR INVITING ME OVER TO SPEAK AT TODAY'S Beijing alumni meeting of the London School of Economics and Political Science. First off, I have a confession to make. I applied to the LSE more than a decade ago, but without any luck. So I consider this meeting with you today as a dream come true. Therefore, I salute you for being able to live and study at this great institution.

Next, let me start with my own experience with the *Financial Times*. A few months ago, Lionel Barber, chief editor of the newspaper, paid an official visit to the Chongyang Institute for Financial Studies, Renmin University of China. In fact, he had just conducted an interview with Premier Li Keqiang that morning prior to making his visit to Chongyang.

At Chongyang, he asked me a question to this effect: "As a new type of think tank, can you influence China's decision-makers?"

I answered: "Yes, of course. We are working hard to increase our influence upon the decision-making process in China."

Throughout the afternoon, the two of us, one of Britain's most powerful media executives and the head of a new Chinese think tank, had a very pleasant conversation. I offered my candid criticism during our conversation: over the past 36 years, most Western media coverage of China has been negative. When future historians look through the stories you published, they will find that you have very little account of the great progress made in China. Aren't you ashamed of that?

He replied: "No! No! We're not like this."

Three weeks later, the *FT* published a story that distorted my research institute as a nationalistic, real estate-funded think tank. And it turned out that it was the *FT*'s only report on Chongyang that year. I really wanted to send a lawyer's letter to the *FT* headquarters in London, but it's no longer necessary now, because it's been sold to the Japanese.

In the light of my own media experience of nearly 10 years, as well as my contacts with the *Financial Times*, I would like to reiterate several of my new ideas about the media in lieu of an introduction to my speech.

First, the global print media is facing a huge crisis. The impact of the internet is an important reason for the current crisis. Over the past 10 years, the proportion of global advertising spending in newspapers halved to 15 per cent, and in magazines it fell from 13 per cent to 7.3 per cent. In China in 2014 alone, more than 30 newspaper and magazine titles either stopped printing or went bankrupt, and the coverage and influence of newspapers and magazines continue to decline. The *New York Times* has confirmed that its paper edition will no longer be available starting from 2016. The nature of the media is changing, and the advent of social media outlets such as Twitter and Facebook has led to a further decline in the status of traditional media. Social media have removed the invisible crown of the uncrowned king of media professionals.

Second, the rapid development of internet technology has transformed communication. It has also highlighted the negativity of the media's role. The media is an important driving force behind political democratization, but it is also an unstable factor in the process of democratization. While people now enjoy more freedom, and more efficient and faster access to information, negative features have also multiplied that are affecting and even threatening our lives in the form of spreading rumors and lies, internet crime, privacy loopholes, money laundering and 'phubbing'. To make matters worse, the highly politicized internet and the fast expansion of individual power have contributed to the rapid agglomeration of like-minded people, which makes it easy for a resistance movement to emerge. The Arab Spring, the riots in London and the Occupy Wall Street movement in 2011 – all of these unrests were fueled by the internet.

Third, China is also impacted by the internet age. Although China must fulfill its democratic mission as a modern country by allowing easy and equal access to information by ordinary Chinese citizens, it must also avoid the shocking impact of information explosion in the post-modern world and keep at bay events similar to the Arab Spring and Occupy Wall Street.

So, when we talk about 'the media, think tanks and political democratization', we actually face a dilemma. On the one hand, we need to recognize the role of the media as the fourth estate, supplementing the three branches of government by providing checks and balances. Yet, the media itself also needs to be checked and balanced, but who will do this and how should it be governed? Unfortunately, discussants involved in the debate over the relationship between Chinese media and political democratization often concentrate on the former. Many people believe that China's media power is suppressed, China has what they call a 'propaganda department' or a 'censorship' system, and some even think that China is not different from the former Soviet system. In my opinion, this view is not only wrong, but also biased, or at least they do not understand the complexity of China.

Stop looking at China's changes through the lens of ideology

A few years ago, I asked Bob Woodward, one of the famous *Washington Post* reporters who covered the Watergate affair: "Bob, did the White House call to stop you from what you're doing?"

Bob, in his sixties, immediately replied: "No! Never! " Then, a few seconds later, he whispered: "But they did call my boss."

Some of you in the audience today might argue by saying it's called spin or political cover-up, which is different from Chinese media censorship. Well, then, how about this: a demonstration on the street. In the West it's called a 'riot' but if it happens abroad it's a 'revolution'. And what about illegal violence: it's called 'terrorism' in the United States and 'silent resistance' in China. Can that be anything but double standards?

It is my sincere hope that, when we talk about the Chinese media, think tanks and the process of democratization, the first thing we should do is to stop reverting to ideology, not to mention double standards. Several decades ago, there were numerous entries in the lexicon of the Chinese media and think tanks, such as 'American imperialism', 'capitalism' and so on. However, that is no longer the case, while there are still plenty of ideological terms reserved for dealing with China in the Western media.

So long as it can stop looking at China through an ideological lens, we should be able to reach such a consensus between China and the West. First, both Chinese and Western media professionals work hard and are part of the social elite, though it is difficult for both of them to perform their duties. Second, both Chinese and Western media have many demerits and shortcomings, although they are all playing their own social roles. Third, both Chinese and Western media are inextricably linked to their governments, although the degrees to which they are linked vary. The value of the media to the political process lies not in whether the country concerned is communist or has a multi-party electoral system, but in whether it can perform its own social functions.

China currently has 1m media professionals, which is 2.5 times more than the total number of media professionals of the 25 countries in the European Union. It is about four times the 54 countries in Africa. They are among the best and brightest social groups in China. A considerable number of them, with the utmost responsibility and integrity, dig into every ugly event in our society, in an attempt to push China forward, in much the same way as American muckraking journalists did in the early twentieth century, who helped usher in the Progressive Era. Some of them worked hard to share China's success story with the world, hoping to promote the Chinese media's discursive power. A large proportion of them are working at local levels, in counties and cities, covering interesting events out there on the streets, as well as entertainment and gossip, news on business developments, and pitching local events to a national audience and readership. More important, China also has 3.5m websites and 600m internet users, most of whom are active users of Weibo and WeChat. They send messages to each other, express their love for the things they love, demonstrate their indignation at social vices, show sympathy for those caught in tragic events, and express their longing for the good and beautiful. Of course, it remains a challenge for China to deal with all the rumors, fraud and crime that are associated with the internet. Therefore, it is imperative for the Chinese government to turn the original propaganda system into a media governance system so as to adapt to the changing situation of the internet age.

Like many developed countries, China lacks the experience of governance in the information age. A lot of policy implementation and case handling inevitably leads to controversy and criticism. But we must say that, up to now, mankind has not found a proper way to govern society in the internet age. From this point of view, the role of the Chinese media to facilitate political governance is threefold: to disseminate information, to publicize the good and beautiful, and to denounce the ugly and evil. Unfortunately, in Western studies of China's media, there is only a one-dimensional narrative that is either 'political censorship' or 'media resistance against government control', which ignores the real existence of 1m Chinese media professionals and 600m

WeChat users. It simplifies the complexity of a country in which millions of stories are happening in every corner of the land.

In China, media is the main entity of state governance and a major contributor to national development, social stability and economic reform. It also subjects itself to state governance, acting out the role of gatekeeper, committed to preventing the general public from being overwhelmed with information that may cause political turmoil in China. Furthermore, Chinese media ensures the exchange of information that is necessary for 1.4bn people to interact with one another so that public opinion can be expressed, but importantly, not in an extremist fashion, because extremism leads to political disorder and social unrest. In fact, this is actually the third way for media to develop in China, a path of incrementalism for Chinese media and political democratization to take.

How can think tanks better serve decision-making?

In the process of political democratization, the issue is not freedom deprivation of the general public; instead, it is the issue of pluralism and complexity. So, what constitutes authentic public opinion needs to be screened and analyzed by professional institutions. In fact, this is the background against which the new type of think tank emerges. Since he took office in 2013, President Xi Jinping has attached great importance to the role of new think tanks. His administration wrote the establishment of think tanks into the CPC Central Committee's highest directives of the Third Plenary Session of the 18th CPC Party Congress.

At present, there are almost 400 think tanks in China. Over the past two years, more than 200 new think tanks have been founded in the country, equivalent to the total number of British think tanks in existence. What is more interesting is that national-level media outlets such as *People's Daily*, Xinhua News Agency, Sina.com and Phoenix New Media have also launched their own think tanks. The most important role of think tanks is to identify problems and provide solutions to decision-makers. In fact, almost all Chinese government agencies consult think tanks for professional advice when drafting documents. Take my institution, for example: Chongyang Institute for Financial Studies, Renmin University of China, has strong communications and research teams. We receive invitations almost every day, many of them from various government departments, and our research results are disseminated through internal references, reports, newsletters, columns, interviews and so on, providing advice to senior officials as well as informing and enlightening the general public. This comprehensive strength has enabled our organization to rank among the 'top 150 global think tanks' within two years of its inception. The accomplishment we achieved at Chongyang reflects the latest changes in think tank building, as well as the trend of convergence between media and think tanks, which has a long-term impact on China's political democratization. Unfortunately, 'what exactly think tanks should do' has yet to be further explained in China. The term 'think tank' has been around for about 100 years. It originated in the military word 'tank', implying that powerful thought should be as aggressive as a tank.

In fact, the world is exploring how to operate a think tank. I have visited almost all of the world's most famous think tanks on my research tours. Numerous articles have been published in English language newspapers to criticize the development of American think tanks. In August last year, the *New York Times* published a lengthy piece to criticize the status quo that exists in American think tanks. Regarding this issue, I presented the question I had been obsessed with to Dr. Henry Kissinger, whom I met at one point in my life: "Why does America have so many famous think tanks, and yet they fail to prevent the United States, the only superpower, from declining? Have America's strategies for the past two decades all been wrong?"

However, in three respects China's think tanks are not doing as well as their counterparts in the US. One is that China's think tanks have not yet developed into an industry. There are more than 1,800 think tanks in the US, far more than in China. Second, Chinese think tank researchers are not professional enough. In US think tanks, there are those who specialize in media relations and government relations. Chinese think tank researchers tend to be 'Jacks of all trades, masters of none'. Third, Chinese think tanks are not professional enough. If China can operate its think tanks the way the US does, I believe that China's think tanks will also play a bigger role.

Media, think tanks and the democratization process in China

To observe China's democratization, which is a global concern now, we should follow the logic of inquisitive and dynamic thinking. Twenty-five years ago, the American scholar Francis Fukuyama said that the real history of the world had just begun. The same is true of how to govern the media in the internet age and how to improve the performance of think tanks. By the same token, we, as think tank professionals, have just begun to accumulate the necessary experience.

In the course of human progress, we are never entitled to think that we know everything. In recent years, many American scholars have been arrogant enough to argue that the world should have one model, the American model. But historical evidence shows that the American model has stalled global development in the early 21st century. While in the past 37 years of reform and opening up, though China has been open for criticism, it has, on the whole, made the fewest mistakes in the world and has made no irreversible strategic mistakes. The development-related experience of such a big country merits global attention and research effort. I visited the LSE a few years ago, and I was most impressed by the fact that this famous university was founded by a group of thinkers who believed in Fabianism. They believe that it is possible to achieve socialism through moderate improvement and gradualism. This trend of thought and method is still of great significance to present day China.

China has implemented the most thorough reform programs in the history of mankind. Yet it will not follow the historical path of the former Soviet Union or the present path of the US. That China is pressing ahead with a different path remains a subject that I hope to discuss further with the professors and student body at the LSE.

II

'REVERSE GLOBALIZATION' IS AN ILLUSION, WHILE GLOBAL GOVERNANCE HAS A FUTURE

THE GLOBAL GOVERNANCE 'REVOLUTION' HAS NOT YET BEEN ACCOMPLISHED

Normally, when the world economy is sick, the prescriptions given by the West are 'take the medicine', 'take the medicine' and then 'take the medicine'. The idea is to target only those places where it hurts. What about Chinese prescriptions? They involve analyzing why things have not improved despite having taken so many drugs for so many years. If things don't get better, other new remedies should be prescribed, because we should not rely on medicine alone. To put it in traditional Chinese medical terms, we should depend on long-term nourishment, open the passages through which vital energy circulates, activate blood circulation to dissipate blood stasis, dredge the meridian bone and effect a radical cure. To put it in modern-day terms, 'innovation, vitality, linkage and inclusion' are four such long-term prescriptions.

China is Speaking *is a popular television show, produced by Southeast Satellite TV, which is now airing at prime time throughout China. Dr. Wang Wen was invited to speak on the show near the end of 2016.*

Thanks to *China is Speaking* for giving me the opportunity to share the story of global governance and China's contribution to this movement.

November 13, 2015, on the first day of the official opening of the G20 Summit in Antalya, Turkey, Chongyang Institute for Financial Studies, Renmin University of China, co-hosted the G20 preheat summit at the summit venue with our partners. At one point, a Turkish government official pulled me aside and handed me an invitation.

He said: "Our Prime Minister, Ahmet Davutoglu, would like to invite you to a welcome dinner for state leaders who are to participate in tomorrow's G20 Summit. You are one of the only two representatives from global think tanks, and the only representative from a Chinese think tank."

Wang Wen at the G20 Summit press conference in Antalya, Turkey, November 16, 2015

At the dinner reception, I briefed the president of South Africa, the president of Indonesia, the prime minister of Malaysia and the president of Azerbaijan on the development of the Chinese think tank. Former UN Secretary General Kofi Annan said to me: "China has done a great job." Indian Prime Minister Narendra Modi said: "China, very good." The prime minister of Canada, the young and energetic Justin Trudeau, gave me a hug and said: "Let's take a selfie."

That day, I was so very proud of China's participation in global governance, and I felt the power and glory of being involved in such a great undertaking as a young think tank scholar.

You may ask what exactly we have done to receive this kind of royal treatment? Permit me to begin with the concept of global governance. 'Global governance' is a concept that came into being only two or three decades ago. In the past, the predominant way to promote globalization was through military rule or colonization, while after the second world war, global affairs were increasingly governed by institutions, rules and consultation. Unfortunately, over a long period of time, the rules of the world were made predominantly by seven Western countries headed by the US. Therefore, financial, trade, investment and other aspects of the international rules of operation were formulated in favor of Western countries. It was not until after the international financial crisis in 2008 that the G7 countries, the EU, China, India and 12 other emerging economies gathered in Washington at the proposal of the then US President George W Bush. This was the first G20 Summit. At this point, for the first time in human history, representatives from both Western and non-Western countries and developing countries had come together at this annual event. It finally put emerging economies on a par with the developed world.

The G20 summit, which took place in 2008, has made an important contribution to the recovery of the global economy, but the world has not fully recovered from the global economic crisis. Let me give you a simple example: the global economy grew at an average rate of 4.5 per cent between 2000 and 2007, followed by negative growth in 2008/09 as the crisis bottomed out. The recovery began after 2009, but it was weak. The average global growth rate between 2010 and 2014 was 3.5 per cent, falling to 3.2 per cent in 2015. In 2016, it was expected to be only 3 per cent. In contrast, China's economy, despite experiencing a slight weakening in growth, retained the most growth potential in the global economy. For years, China has maintained a growth rate of between 6.5 per cent and 9 per cent.

At this crucial juncture, the world is expecting China to provide a 'China solution' for global economic growth. Since 2013, Chongyang Institute for Financial Studies, Renmin University of China, has started to research the G20 in order to promote China's bid for the 2016 G20

Summit. Party and state leaders have highly praised our work. In 2016 in particular, we were appointed the China coordinator think tank for G20. We managed to host high profile public events in 10 cities around the world, such as a grand G20 think tank meeting, various book launches, as well as policy recommendations and international communications, events to raise public opinion and media briefings. In the process, we understand the effectiveness and appeal of the 'China solution' for global governance. It is known that the theme of China's G20 Summit this year is 'Toward an innovative, invigorated, interconnected and inclusive world economy', which is simply called the 'four I's' in English. Turkey proposed 'three I's' for the previous G20 Summit – investment for growth, inclusiveness and implementation. Some Western scholars responded to this by saying that they should add another 'I', which is *impossible.*

Why? One reason is that Turkey lacks the authority and strength to propose global economic governance in the eyes of the West. Another reason is that investment as a solution to growth, which in itself is still a continuation of stimulus in the 'Western rescue package', has proved to be a bad way out.

What are China's four prescriptions to reverse the global economic downturn?

The first one, of course, is 'innovation'. This requires thinking outside the box, instead of sticking to the rules and regulations. It further means that we should pursue technological and institutional innovation. It involves pressing ahead with intensified reform efforts in the international financial, trade and economic systems, promoting the construction of global infrastructure and building a global innovation system. There is no possibility for economic growth without innovation. At the G20 Summit in Hangzhou, China creatively worked with other participants to reach a consensus on 29 major global issues, which in itself was a big accomplishment in innovation.

A few weeks ago, I attended an international conference in Washington DC. I told my US counterparts that Americans tend to emphasize 'innovation' in terms of science and technology, whereas for China 'innovation' is more associated with institutional innovation. Without significant reform and innovation, I'm afraid it's hard for the world to escape the economic downturn. China needs reform and opening up, and so does the US. Some of my American colleagues agree with me.

Why then 'invigoration'? The idea is that there should be a more dynamic and global flow of goods, people, technology and resources in order to resist rising trade and investment protectionism, to expand market opportunities for the development of various countries so that the global economy will not lose its vitality. For developing countries, it is particularly important to invigorate their economic vitality.

In this regard, China achieved the following at the G20 summit in Hangzhou: developing various guiding principles for strengthening trade and investment to promote cross-border e-commerce; rallying more developing countries to participate in the global trading system; and guiding the world to build a more dynamic and open trading and investment system. Compared with some conservative voices in Europe and the US, China's 'invigoration' plan can facilitate global economic recovery.

Third, 'interconnected'. The idea is to break down barriers and achieve worldwide infrastructure connectivity, involving roads, electricity supply and the internet. China is well aware that developing countries are still lagging behind developed countries, but that developed economies are not performing well either. The key to progress lies in the huge technological, institutional and infrastructure barriers to trade, investment and the allocation of resources.

A few months ago, I was on a research trip in Kenya, where Chinese companies built Kenya's first railway in a century, from Mombasa to Nairobi. Local residents are looking forward to the future with great anticipation and are grateful to China for its contribution to their development. It turns out that, the more infrastructure you build, the greater the chance your economy will develop. 'To get rich, build roads first' is a form of best practice that China is happily sharing with the rest of the world.

What, then, is 'inclusiveness'? It means allowing more poor people to enjoy the dividends of development. We should be aware that the global average of the Gini coefficient, which measures inequality, has reached about 0.7, which exceeds the accepted 'red line' of 0.6. More than half a century has passed since the creation of several dozen newly independent countries, which originally were developing countries founded through national liberation movements during and after the second world war. They remain developing countries. They have never prospered. In future, the world cannot keep developing countries poor, since they account for four fifths of the world's population. Proposed and promoted by China, the United Nations Conference on Sustainable Development Agenda, including the 17 major goals set by the CPC with an aim to eradicate poverty and illiteracy, has become, for the first time, an important agenda for the G20 Summit. At China's invitation, the summit attracted the largest number of delegates from developing countries. As a consequence, voices from more developing countries were heard, large countries could reach out to help small countries, countries that prospered first could support those lagging behind, thus promoting the formation of a community of common interests and shared destiny.

Let me make an analogy here. Normally, when the world economy is sick, the prescription given by the West is 'take the medicine', 'take the medicine' and 'take the medicine', the idea being to target only those places where it hurts. And what about the Chinese prescription? Well, the Chinese prescription is to analyze why things have not improved after taking so many drugs for so many years? If things don't get better, new remedies should be prescribed, because we should not rely on medicine alone. To put it in traditional Chinese medical terms, we should depend on long-term nourishment, open the passages through which vital energy circulates, activate blood circulation to dissipate blood stasis, dredge the meridian bone and effect a radical cure. To put it in modern-day terms, 'innovative, invigorated, interconnected and inclusive' are four such prescriptions for long-term sickness.

The four prescriptions not only inherit the spirit of internationalism in Mao Zedong's time, but also share China's successful experience with the world. They enrich Deng Xiaoping's theory of "seeking truth from facts, and practice is the only criterion for testing truth". They also draw on the cultural wisdom in Chinese tradition: 'Do not impose on others what you do not desire others to impose upon you.'

The G20 Summit has been an unprecedented success, and China's proposals for global governance have received unprecedented support. Why? Because China has made a great contribution to the development of the world for a long time, and the world is grateful for its contribution.

I sum up three specific contributions: contributions to the world economy, international peace and global politics.

China's contribution to the world economy

In terms of the UN's goal of reducing poverty in the world, China has contributed about 90 per cent of total global poverty reduction. In other words, the vast majority of those people who have been lifted out of poverty over the past 30 years or so are from China. A China that is getting richer first is reaching out to help those who are becoming rich later. China's economy has contributed more than a third of annual global net growth over the past decade. 'Made-in-China' allows the world easy access to products of good quality and low price. For developing countries, the benefits of free trade with China are far more beneficial than the so-called 'political democracy' offered by the West. China's infrastructure-oriented foreign investment has greatly improved the livelihood of people from around the world. I have been to dozens of countries in the developing world, including in Asia, Africa and Latin America, where I have witnessed the efforts of the Chinese who are quietly improving the well-being of local people in their respective countries. Since the second world war, formerly colonized countries that won independence through national liberation movements have been working to upgrade themselves from low-income to high-income countries, but only one country succeeded, Japan, which turned out to be financed by the US.

It is a great shame that the West governed the world for more than half a century, the result being that the rich have become richer and the poor have become poorer. But thanks to China's economic contribution, poor countries are likely to make a comeback.

These days, many institutions are celebrating the 15th anniversary of China's entry into the WTO. Fifteen years ago, global trade totaled US$12.5tn, and now it stands at about US$16tn; fifteen years ago, China's total trade volume was about US$600bn, and now it is about US$4tn, leapfrogging from the seventh largest trading nation to the largest trading nation in the world. Based on the numbers, we can see that the absolute increase in global trade volume in the past 15 years is just about the same as China's trade growth. It is the increase in China's foreign trade that has boosted global trade and made the most significant contribution to the new round of globalization.

China's contribution to world peace

If China's economic contribution is more about improving human livelihoods, then China's other contributions relate to the protection of human life. China has been the only major country in the world that has not waged a war over the past 30 years. It is admirable for China to stand firm as an advocate for peaceful settlement of international disputes. It is widely known that the rise of Western powers has always been accompanied by war. There were countless wars fought during the middle and late 19th century, which was known as the 'reshuffle period' for countries to emerge as great powers. Larger conflicts included the Opium War in 1840, the Crimean War in 1853, the annexation of Indochina by France in 1858, the Second Opium War in 1860, the various wars that allowed Western powers to divide the whole of Africa, and the War of 1898 between America and Spain. The rise of the West was a process of blood and fire, guns and cannons.

What's worse, in order to transfer the crisis and stabilize the nation, Western European countries were able to export the jobless to Africa, exile prisoners to Australia and send heathens to the Americas, exchange opium for silver in Asia and enjoy the fruits of modernization all to themselves. At that time, the population of the whole Western world could be measured in terms of tens of millions, but China today has 1.3bn people. China successfully controls its domestic issues within its own borders and does not export its refugees, disasters, famine, war or diseases to the world. No doubt, China's greatest contribution to world peace is that it manages to maintain peace and stability in a country whose population accounts for one fifth of the world's total. Think of the wars in Kosovo, Afghanistan, Iraq, Libya, Syria and so on that the US has provoked or participated in over the past 20 years. Millions of people have died, and millions of families have been displaced. Thus, it is all the more necessary to congratulate China for its contribution to world peace.

In addition, China has acceded to almost all the conventions on maintaining world peace, making it the country with one of the largest number of peacekeeping troops. As a permanent member of the United Nations, China, in cooperation with other countries, emphasizes the use of multilateralism to resolve conflicts, making outstanding contributions to the peaceful resolution of conflicts in the world.

As Germany's former chancellor, Helmut Schmidt, said: "Throughout its history, China has never established a colony in other countries. Foreign policy-wise, China has never had the tradition of seizing the territory of other countries. China is by far the most peaceful power in world history. It will not turn its back on this great tradition of peaceful rise." This is by far the most typical commentary on China's contribution to peace enshrined in the Chinese Dream.

China's contributions to global politics

More than 20 years ago, the Cold War ended with the triumph of Western-style capitalism over communism. The whole world gave three loud cheers to 'the end of history, celebrating Western liberal democracy as the final form of human government'.

However, more than 20 years later, the international financial crisis has laid bare fatal flaws in Western economic regulatory policy, and the 'Occupy' movements that swept the world have highlighted a major crisis in liberal democratic institutions. After the third wave of the liberal democracy movement, the building of democratic institutions in developing countries has been stagnant, and various trends of thoughts have emerged and compete against one another.

Wang Jisi, a renowned Chinese expert on international issues, said that the basic trend of world political development reflects the complexity and multifaceted nature of the political structure and process of various countries. "A new chapter in world history may just begin to unfold." Currently, more and more scholars in the West are rethinking their own systems and are acknowledging the merits of China's incremental reform program. Francis Fukuyama, the author of *The End of History and the Last Man*, has admitted in recent years that "there is nothing the United States can teach China about democracy". Therefore, in a political sense, the rise of China provides another option for the development of the new world history. Democracy has no unified model and no unique form. The present reality shows that the separation of powers and the system of two or multiple parties are not fixed political reform options. China, both an ancient and modern country, can draw upon its time-honored ancient wisdom to improve its domestic politics and governance. This empirical model of political reform is, as part of its Chinese Dream, the pinnacle that China can contribute to world politics.

Wang Wen greets Nirendra Modi, India's prime minister, at the G20 Summit in Antalya, Turkey, November 19, 2015

Such huge contributions to world economy, peace and politics are made through years of hard work and by millions and millions of Chinese people. We should treasure and feel proud of the great accomplishments. I have been to nearly 50 countries and covered almost all major powers in my career as a journalist. In future, I hope to be able to travel around the world, especially to the remaining 200 countries so that I can write more about China's rise, the single most wonderful event of the 21st century.

The Chinese are now looked up to when we travel in various parts of the world, instead of being ridiculed as the 'sick men of East Asia' or the 'yellow peril' of a hundred years ago. This is a hard-won achievement. However, I feel reserved in my optimism. Some of us are not confident enough when talking about China's contribution to the world. Clearly, China has made many contributions, but we're still too shy to share, or because of low self-esteem, we do not dare to say, or we will not say it. On the other hand, Western public opinion has not yet acknowledged China's contribution, refusing to cover its development and contribution in an objective fashion. To complicate matters, the 'China collapse theory' and 'China threat theory' remain wildly popular, unfortunately. Therefore, continued efforts must be made to reform the international governance system.

In the 30 years following the founding of the PRC in 1949, China managed to resist foreign aggression; during the second 30-year period, it managed to solve the problem of feeding its own population. Since we're now entering the third 30-year period, I am afraid that the issue is how to resist the notorious China-bashing.

So, to paraphrase Dr. Sun Yat-sen's famous adage, the revolution in global governance is not yet complete; let's work harder.

We look forward to the day when the system of global governance truly represents justice, reason and peace, instead of a utopia, or an illusory dream, but an ideal that needs to be real and worthy of all mankind's struggle. As a rising power, China is making its due contribution to this ideal.

'REVERSE GLOBALIZATION' IS AN ILLUSION, CHINA IS SET TO LEAD THE NEW ERA OF GLOBALIZATION

Opposition to globalization has arisen in the face of economic difficulties across the world, as well as security issues, such as refugee and regional conflicts, and social problems, such as widening income disparities and unemployment. However, the trend of globalization has not been reversed but instead has been exaggerated by the 'losing end' of globalization via the internet in the public opinion game. China has benefited from the development of globalization, and in future it will lead the path of new globalization.

There has been a rising wave of opposition to globalization across the globe since 2016. Against that background, Dr. Wang Wen was invited on lecture tours in Chile, Peru, Kenya and India. This paper reflects his new thinking on the issue of 'reverse globalization'. The original article in Chinese was published in Reference News *on March 15, 2017. The English version was published in the* Financial Times *on April 10, 2017.*

THERE HAS BEEN A RISING WAVE OF OPPOSITION TO GLOBALIZATION ACROSS the world. From widespread trade protectionism to slow trade growth and tightened immigration policies, it would seem that the world is facing a backlash against globalization. However, data and theoretical deduction tell a different story: economic globalization is still the norm. In fact, the engine of globalization has shifted from developed to emerging economies. Therefore, the latter should continue to open up their markets and seize the opportunities the next round of globalization will bring. For decades, anti-globalization movements have emerged intermittently, impacting global progress. Western economists have already provided an interpretation of the coexisting globalization and anti-globalization phenomenon.

In this light, the current anti-globalization wave is more like a regional and cyclical relapse at this particular phase among Western countries. Though the West has great influence on the world, rising powers seem to perceive globalization quite differently.

In addition, from a mid- and long-term point of view, data indicate that the influence of the West might be impaired. Trade, as a percentage of GDP, in the world remained steady from 2011 to 2015.

Though there has been a modest slowdown in the global trade of goods denominated in dollars, a large part of this decline could be proven to be a 'statistical illusion' given the impact of dollar strength and overlapping factors, such as decreasing US dependence on foreign energy and the long-term low price of commodities.

Moreover, in the seven years after the 2008 financial crisis, the global service trade grew faster than GDP, and the contribution of service trade to GDP climbed from 12.5 per cent in 2008 to 13 per cent in 2015, serving as an important force for boosting global economic growth and increasing employment.

In capital flows, global foreign direct investment is also recovering robustly. Though it dropped to US$1.2tn in 2014, it quickly bounced back to US$1.76tn in 2015 – the highest level seen since the crisis.

Global transnational mergers and acquisitions amounted to US$4.9tn in 2015, surpassing the 2007 level of US$4.6tn and providing hard evidence of the expansion of multinational corporations in the context of globalization.

It is evident that there have been doubts about and opposition to globalization in the face of global economic difficulties and risks. These include security issues, such as refugee and regional conflicts, and social problems, such as widening income disparities and unemployment. However, the trend of globalization has not been reversed. It is indeed exaggerated by the 'losing end' of globalization via the internet in the public opinion game.

Concerns in the West

The anti-globalization sentiments in the West can be seen on the surface in policy. Western countries pursue self-protection as their competitive edge diminishes in today's world, and the underlying reasons could be threefold.

For one, the sentiments are the result of the overlapping effect of intensified internal contradictions and the negative influence of globalization. Globalization is a 'double-edged sword', which means that, in the competitive logic of relative gains, it will inevitably produce winners and losers.

Labor distribution and production outsourcing in the global industrial chain coupled with technological progress has led to the relocation of manufacturing industry, which forms the core of the real economy, to the developing countries. The middle and lower classes in developed countries have lost jobs or seen reductions in pay, so they are the 'losers' in globalization.

At the same time, the internet is a magnifier of negative public opinion, so anxiety and anger, like infectious diseases, spread rapidly, and the situation has been exacerbated by the refugee crisis in Europe and the threat of terrorism. All these factors have conspired to create a large audience for politicians willing to exploit public discontent.

Next, rising powers, including China, are making the West nervous. While the emerging economies show more interest and capacity to participate in global governance, the West, worn down by the crisis, is declining and withdrawing from the world stage.

Against this backdrop, Western commentators have argued that traditional globalization has come to an end, and a new trade system should be put in place, such as a regional trade mechanism, that serves their interest and keeps them on top of the game.

The anti-globalization narratives are in the end looking for ways to maximize national interest in the process of globalization. Globalization, as a scholar in the West put it, should continue out of 'each nation's free will'.

New round of globalization

The progress of social productivity and technology means the trend of globalization is irreversible. However, due to the differences in national resources and policy orientations, globalization has created some negative outcomes. Therefore, the old system of globalization, which has been dominated by developed Western countries, cannot meet the current demand. As a consequence, an upgrade in global governance and a transformation of globalization as well as a new round of globalization is imminent.

Chinese President Xi Jinping's speech at Davos in January attracted global attention. To an extent, his main ideas chart the path of new globalization: develop a dynamic, innovation-driven growth model; pursue a well-coordinated and inter-connected approach to develop a model of open, mutually beneficial co-operation; develop a balanced, equitable and inclusive development model.

Certainly, the undertaking will not be easy and there are at least two major issues to be tackled.

The first task is to challenge backward global governance concepts. The bankruptcy of neoliberalism and the Washington Consensus requires new ideas to solve the internal problems in developed countries as well as the shortage of global public goods and the dislocation between common interests and national interests.

Non-traditional threats have a spillover effect due to the generalization of global governance issues, rampant terrorism, energy and food security crises, and the spread of infectious diseases. However, the present multilateral system and bilateral coping mechanism are incompatible and fragmented, breeding a variety of risks and crises. On this basis, this is a call for grand ideas in the current era.

Second, existing global security, trade and financial mechanisms, such as the UN, the WTO and the IMF, are struggling to respond to the ongoing crisis around the world. The need to reform the original mechanism and reshape global governance rules, in accordance with the latest international structure, is increasing. Developing countries need to be better included in the decision-making process in order to ultimately safeguard the implementation and authority of the global mechanism.

Belt and Road initiative

China benefits from the development of globalization and open economy that facilitates trade and investment. Against this backdrop, we have seen something unprecedented in recent years. From the G20 Hangzhou summit and the Apec Lima summit to the coming 'Belt and Road' summit this May, Chinese leaders, government officials, businessmen and scholars have been seen at every occasion trying to convince their Western counterparts to be confident in globalization.

The new round of globalization China has proposed emphasizes that all countries have equal opportunities to participate, regardless of their size and strength, and share the positive results of globalization through trade exchanges and investment co-operation.

Global governance should reasonably reflect the demands of all parties in terms of rules and concepts, and though major powers provide global public goods, all countries are bound to share the fruits and benefits fairly.

It is foreseeable that the West will continue be cautious towards the process of globalization, but the development of a new model of globalization needs its participation to push forward from a global community of common interests to a community of common destiny.

In the absence of global economic and financial public goods, the Belt and Road initiative has become the largest public product provided by a rising China, which embodies its main idea of promoting economic openness in the new era.

To conclude, in response to rising anti-globalization sentiments, we should really embrace a new era of globalization.

COUNTRIES OF THE WORLD, UNITE! LET'S BUILD A LONG-TERM GOVERNANCE MECHANISM

Countries around the world were threatened by the financial crisis in 2008 due to the financial tsunami that originated in the US. In a spirit of sincere partnership, the G20 has strengthened coordination and cooperation in macroeconomic policies and succeeded in defusing the short-term risks posed by the global financial crisis, creating the resultant force of global economic growth.

The G20 Think Tank Forum was held at the Brookings Institution in Washington DC on April 13, 2016. Representatives of more than 40 think tanks from around the world attended the forum. Dr. Wang Wen delivered a keynote speech.

THE IMPORTANCE OF THE G20 REMAINS THE SAME AS IT WAS BACK IN 2008. G20 countries should seek a convergence of forces to build a long-term governance mechanism to deal with the current new growth trap in the global economy.

The reasons are as follows:

Major agencies have slashed their predictions for global growth. The forecast for global growth for 2016 has been lowered to 2.9 per cent. It will be the second year in a row that the global economy has grown at under 3 per cent, well below expectations, after 2.4 per cent in 2015. Please keep in mind that real global GDP growth averaged 3.26 per cent annually from 2008 to 2014. At the G20 Leaders' Summit in Brisbane, Australia, the G20 countries set a goal to increase the overall global economy by more than 2 per cent by the end of 2018. It seems that the goal set by the G20 countries will fail. This is because, in order to achieve that goal, the global economy needs to grow at an average of more than 3.2% from 2015 to 2018.

Currently, expectations of Federal Reserve rate hikes are gradually forming, as clearly as a 'sword of Damocles' that hangs above efforts to rebalance the global economy, posing a potential threat to the validity of G20 policy co-ordination. In particular, since August 2015, speculation about the Fed's rate rise has mounted, triggering global financial market turmoil and a large outflow of arbitrage capital from emerging markets. Excessive exchange rate fluctuations and disorderly adjustment in many countries have seriously affected regional, and even global, economic and financial stability. Commodity prices have continued to fall and global deflationary pressures have emerged, with complex implications for global rebalancing against the backdrop of increased downside risks and vulnerabilities to the global economy. The sharp fall in commodity prices has added to the downward pressure on emerging market economies such as Russia and Brazil that are heavily dependent on commodity exports. The recovery in developed countries such as the US, European nations and Japan has been weak. Major currencies have depreciated against the dollar and exchange rates have fluctuated sharply. The IMF also cut its estimate for US economic growth from 2.6 per cent to 2.4 per cent in 2016, while the eurozone's economic growth forecast for 2016 was cut to 1.5 per cent from 1.7 per cent, and Japan's forecast down to 0.5 per cent from 1 per cent.

Global trade protectionism is on the rise and the engine of economic growth is waning. Total global trade fell nearly 14 per cent in 2015 from a year earlier according to WTO data. In 2016, global trade will grow by 3.9 per cent, still below the average of 5 per cent over the past 20 years.

In short, because of the nature of the 'growth trap' of the second 10-year period in the 21st century, the global economy has a 'new' growth trap. This includes the aging population among major economies, the 'new gap' in global wealth distribution, the 'middle obstruction' of global technological innovation and geopolitical risk.

The world faced the threat of a worldwide financial crisis in 2008 due to the financial tsunami. That year, driven by the needs of world economic development, developed countries and emerging economies held the first G20 Summit in Washington, DC, in order to strengthen dialogue and policy coordination. The G20 mechanism came into being and became the primary forum of global economic cooperation. The G20, in a spirit of sincere partnership, has strengthened coordination and cooperation in macroeconomic policies, in an effort to defuse the short-term risks posed by the global financial crisis, creating a convergence of forces for global economic growth.

One should caution, however, that the differences in economic trends and policy orientations of major countries make it more difficult to coordinate G20 macro policies. The US economy is recovering, slowly pressing the 'austerity' button, whereas the eurozone and Japan need to maintain extremely loose monetary policies in order to stimulate their economies. This seriously divided economic situation and monetary policy orientations have caused severe shocks in international financial markets, which have exposed the global economy to the risk of imbalance, and even a growth dilemma.

Expectations of the Fed's raising of interest rates add to the complexity and difficulty of G20 policy coordination. The US, a major player in the world economy, needs to take full account of the implications for other countries in formulating macroeconomic policies. G20 members account for more than 80 per cent of the total global economy and have an unshirkable responsibility for world economic growth. It is necessary to strengthen macroeconomic policy communication and coordination, and to jointly formulate policies and take joint actions in order to prevent negative spillover effects, maintain financial market stability, promote investment and consumption, and jointly boost world economic growth.

THE TTIP AND TPP WILL GO DOWN IN HISTORY AS A MISTAKE

If the TTIP and TPP are approved by their respective parliaments in the next few years, then two camps will emerge. In that scenario, it is likely that the free trade system and principles that have developed since the end of the second world war will be reshaped. Conflicts and frictions between the new and old rules have added high transaction costs to the development of the world. Differences in trade rules may even lead to conflicts between the two camps.

On February 13, 2016, the International Forum on New Economic Diplomacy was held in Istanbul, Turkey's largest city, where delegates from around the world gathered for a one-day discussion of the Trans-Pacific Strategic Economic Partnership agreement (TPP) and the role of the Transatlantic Trade and Investment Partnership agreement (TTIP) in the current free trade system. Dr. Wang Wen was invited to deliver a keynote speech at the forum as the only representative from China.

First of all, let me take the opportunity, on this sixth day of the Chinese Lunar New Year, to wish you all a happy spring festival according to the traditional Chinese calendar. I'd like to thank the Istanbul Industrial Association for issuing this invitation that allows me travel to Istanbul to share with you a Chinese think tank scholar's views on international trade and the economy. In fact, this is my fourth trip to this great city.

My topic today is free trade and the TTIP. In fact, Chinese scholars tend to discuss TTIP together with another US-promoted trade agreement known as the TPP to analyze changes in international trade patterns. The TPP is expected achieve five main things. First, to establish an exclusive free trade alliance whose rules are more favorable than those of the World Trade Organization (WTO). Second, China's think tank community generally believes that both the TTIP and TPP are becoming WTO 2.0 versions, both of which are initiated and promoted by the US in order to use them as a strategic re-adjustment to strengthen its economic leadership and power to manage international trade. Third, to create a high-quality, high-standard and high-level agreement similar to a free trade agreement. Fourth, to strengthen cross-border institutional coherence rather than focusing on market access standards along the border (such as intellectual property rights, labor, environment, government procurement, SOEs and rules on countries of origin) through trade planning, especially in the hope of emphasizing fair trade rather than free trade. Fifth, to strengthen the flow of trade and trade activities in the global value chain in the distribution of benefits, the re-division of global economic sectors. In other words, both the TTIP and TPP could usher in a new round of revolution in the international economic and trade system. But in terms of current trends, the so-called 'revolution' will not bring about positive gains globally, but will impact the process of transformation of the global order that has developed in a linear fashion, creating a new form of protectionism and unnecessary internal friction in competition between developed and emerging economies, which could in turn lead to larger strategic miscalculations that might harm the global economy, hence heightening tension and uncertainty for various political entities.

My reasons are as follows:

First, the TPP that has been signed and the TTIP agreement, which is expected to be concluded in 2016, runs counter to the strategic intent of the US. The US wants new arrangements for world trade rules to make up for the current drawbacks in international economic organizations and trade negotiations, and a new attempt to circumvent the WTO Doha negotiations. But in fact, the TTIP and TPP are destroying the world economic order it initiated since the second world war in a way that builds a regional trading system of higher standard, especially higher than those within the current WTO system. In other words, the TTIP and TPP are actually ways by which the US rallies Europe and Japan to set up a system of global trade rules in favor of the US and Europe in the name of market liberalization through cross-border economic and trade integration so as to determine technical standards, product specifications and environmental protection indicators. This partly reinforces US leadership in the negotiating process, but ignores the practical effect of, for example, how many new jobs can be created for the US? All this has caused a great deal of debate in the US Congress. The Democratic presidential candidate, Hillary Clinton, has spoken out against it. Republicans are not much interested in it either. Possibilities cannot be ruled out for the next president to repeal or drastically adjust the outcome of the TTIP and TPP negotiations.

Second, the TTIP and TPP exclude nearly all the strong emerging economies, including China, India, Russia, Brazil, Indonesia, the entire Middle East and the whole of Africa. Turkey's accession to the TTIP will depend on its relationship with the European Union. This arrangement of trade rules ignores the voice of emerging economies. If this is not discrimination, then what is? Of course, the US may change the nature of the TTIP and TPP as regional groups and transform them into a future global trade organization. But to achieve that goal, a model of trade transfer and growth must be created, or no other members will join. For now, emerging markets and developing countries are experiencing much faster overall trade growth than TTIP and TPP countries. Is it possible for other countries to join in the context of the high standards set by the TTIP and the TPP? Worse still, the current TTIP and TPP standards are too favorable to developed countries, such as EU members, the US and Japan, thus granting an 'absolute advantage' to developed countries, which will no doubt lead to further inequality in the trading system of the current international economy. In other words, by blocking the global expansion of emerging market economies, the TTIP and the TPP essentially create new trade barriers to protect the interests of developed countries.

Third, as the world's largest trading country and its largest consumer market, China is not included in the TTIP and TPP region, which is often regarded by Chinese scholars as a strategic provocation. But I would rather see it as ignorance. In 2015, China eclipsed the US for the third year in a row as the largest trading country in the world and the largest trading partner in more than 130 countries. In 2015, for the first time, the total transaction volume of China's consumer market surpassed that of the US, with a growth rate 2.5 times greater than that of the US. With the further development of e-commerce in China, along with Chinese economic reform and structural readjustment, as well as the surge in the number of its outbound tourists, China is set to become the world's largest importer in the next five years. In addition, Chinese consumption is becoming a new engine of world economic growth, with China's contribution to global growth at around 35 per cent over the past eight years. The TTIP and TPP set high standards on temporary entry for business professionals, trade in services and principles of origin. It gives the outside world the feeling of an upcoming 'cold war' against trading with China. This is not about promoting globalization; instead, it is a declaration of war against globalization.

So, if you were to ask me or most Chinese economists what they think about the TTIP and TPP, frankly speaking, we would say they are exclusive, not inclusive; they are beneficial to the developed world, but not to the developing world; they are regional, rather than cosmopolitan; they mark a return to protectionism, instead of promoting free trade; they are anti-globalization; they will aggravate trade friction, rather than promote trade settlement.

If the TTIP and TPP were to be approved by the legislative bodies in their respective countries over the next few years, two warring camps might emerge. One would be a trade alliance headed by developed countries in the TTIP and TPP regions. The standards of the alliance are essentially Western in nature, and are 'value trading circles' dominated by Western labor standards, transparency standards, anti-corruption rules and principles of countries of origin. The other is the non-TTIP and TPP region, which is still dominated by the trade system under the existing WTO framework. The difference is that the latter have higher rates of economic contribution, faster growth in trade, stronger development potential and larger populations.

If the two agreements are approved, it is likely that the free trade system and principles that have developed since the end of the second world war will be further reshaped, and the conflicts and frictions between new and old rules will have added higher transaction costs to the development of the world, or there may even be conflicts between the two camps because of differences in trade rules. This is not necessarily what the initiators of the TTIP and TPP negotiations would like to see. Therefore, I suggest that consideration should be given to the future success or failure of the TTIP and TPP and the level of risk involved, thus making corresponding adjustments.

First, maintain trade communication at the global level, particularly at the G20 ministerial level. In 2008, however, after the international financial crisis, the contributions of G7 countries to global economic development started to decline, and the total GDP of emerging economies accounted for more than half of the global total. Coordination among global economies has entered the era of G20. In addition, TTIP and TPP negotiators need to take into account the benefits and needs of G20 members, or emerging economies; otherwise, more countries will be prevented from enjoying the fruits of reciprocal openness.

Second, protect the outcome of free trade negotiations under the framework of the WTO. The Nairobi Conference held in December 2015 advanced the WTO, taking a big step forward in the outcome of the information technology expansion agreement and the agricultural 'export competition'. At the same time, the issues that remain will be more intractable, such as the elimination of tariffs on environmental goods, trade in services agreements and fisheries subsidy agreements. But all negotiators need to further protect and speed up the Doha round negotiation process from the perspective of national and global interests, and promote the global trading system within the WTO framework at the global level.

Third, continue to support the China Regional Economic and Trade Cooperation Network under the Belt and Road initiative. As of the end of 2015, China has signed 14 free trade agreements involving 22 countries and regions, namely China and ASEAN, Singapore, Pakistan, New Zealand, Chile, Peru, Costa Rica, Iceland, Switzerland, South Korea and Australia, plus the Closer Economic Partnership arrangement (CEPA) between the mainland and Hong Kong and Macau, as well as the Framework Agreement on Cross-Strait Economic Cooperation between the mainland and Taiwan. Next, through the Belt and Road initiative, China will promote the free trade zone in the Asia-Pacific region, in Eurasia, as well as the bilateral investment treaty negotiations between China and the US, and various other trade and investment agreements. The principles of all these trade agreements are mutual consultation, construction and sharing, and are truly inclusive of trade, investment, finance and infrastructure investment initiatives.

Compared with the TPP and TTIP, China's Belt and Road initiative has no fixed thresholds or standards, which allows countries to choose appropriate modalities for cooperation in accordance with their level of development and specific national circumstances. This will be more in line with the goal of international economic and trade development, more inclusive and global-oriented, thus creating a community of shared interests, responsibility and the community of shared destiny through the joint efforts of countries along the route, on the basis of respect for diversity so as to build win-win cooperation. The idea, once again, is to ensure that different countries can find points of convergence of interest through cooperation, which is also in line with the actual needs of international economic and trade development and capacity cooperation.

Over the past two years or so, China's trade with, and investment in,

Belt and Road countries has grown faster than elsewhere. This is an initiative worthy of worldwide research and participation. Up to now, more than 70 countries have expressed their enthusiastic support. I trust that Turkish businessmen are benefiting from the Belt and Road initiative. I believe there will be more benefits to come in the foreseeable future.

DEBUNKING TEN MYTHS ABOUT CHINA AND THE SOUTH CHINA SEA

Safeguarding sovereignty and territorial integrity does not necessarily have to involve the use of force. Currently, the most daunting task facing claimant countries involved in the South China Sea disputes is to achieve sustained and rapid development, which requires a peaceful and stable environment, the common denominator to be pursued by countries in the region.

On July 5, 2016, the China-US Think Tank Dialogue on the South China Sea was held in Washington DC. Hosted by the Chongyang Institute for Financial Studies, Renmin University of China, and the Carnegie Foundation for International Peace and organized by the China Research Institute for the South China Sea and the Wilson Center for International Scholars, the dialogue centered on three topics: 'The South China Sea issue: Chinese and US Perspectives', 'Differences and the future: multiple points of view of the South China Sea issue' and 'Ideas and recommendations: a pragmatic solution to the South China Sea issue'. Former Chinese State Councilor Dai Bingguo's remarks in his keynote speech that "the award of the South China Sea arbitration case is nothing more than a piece of trash" has attracted global attention. As a host from the Chinese side, Dr. Wang Wen also made a presentation at the meeting and he published an English article in the South China Morning Post *during the meeting to clarify the top ten myths of the South China Sea issue.*

Throughout its history, the South China Sea has been a 'sea of peace', untouched by a large-scale battle. South China Sea arbitration, however, is turning this region into a powder keg. All too often, public discourse on relations between China and the South China Sea has only made an already complex subject more complicated. There is an urgent need to clarify at least 10 myths.

On July 5, 2016, the author attended a high-profile think tank conference on the South China Sea, with more than 30 former leaders of the US and Chinese governments, along with accomplished scholars from both countries. After the meeting, I felt strongly about the importance of correcting the 10 misperceptions.

Myth One: China's stance against the South China Sea arbitration violates international law. By initiating the arbitration case, the Philippines was the one that broke its own commitment made in the Declaration on the Conduct of Parties in the South China Sea, signed between China and members of the Association of Southeast Asian Nations, which states that disputes should be resolved by those countries directly involved, through friendly consultation and negotiation.

Based on the declaration, China's stance on the arbitration has been firm and clear. It can be summarized as 'non-acceptance, non-participation, non-recognition and non-execution'.

The nature of the dispute involves two separate issues: one is the sovereignty claim over Nansha Islands and the other is maritime rights. Not only are territorial issues beyond the scope of the UN Convention on the Law of the Sea, China had also lodged a declaration with the UN in 2006 – in accordance with Article 298 of the Law of the Sea – that it does not accept any of the compulsory dispute settlement procedures with regard to disputes on maritime delimitation. Thus, neither can the Philippines initiate a compulsory arbitration under this convention, nor does the Permanent Court of Arbitration at The Hague have the jurisdiction to adjudicate on the case.

The conduct of the Philippines violates the fourth article of the Declaration on the Conduct of Parties, abuses the Law of the Sea arbitration procedures and infringes China's right to choose the means of dispute settlement. It is thus illegal.

Myth Two: The 'nine-dash line' does not comply with the Law of the

Sea. The accusation does not hold any water. To begin with, the nine-dash line predated the Law of the Sea. In 1948, for example, the Chinese government published the dotted line to reaffirm China's sovereignty and relevant rights in the South China Sea. In addition, the convention does not exclude historical rights; its repeated references to 'historical bays' and 'historical titles' speak volumes about its respect for historical rights.

No country, including China, claims sovereignty over the whole South China Sea.

Furthermore, the preamble of the Law of the Sea mentions the desirability to "establish through this Convention, with due regard for the sovereignty of all states, a legal order for the seas and oceans". This makes clear that the issue of territorial sovereignty is not subject to the Law of the Sea. Therefore, it cannot be used as a basis to judge China's nine-dash line.

Myth Three: China claims sovereignty over the whole South China Sea. Incorrect media reports have contributed to this misunderstanding. The fact is, no country, including China, claims sovereignty over the whole South China Sea. The core of the South China Sea issue relates to the disputes over sovereignty and maritime administration of parts of Nansha Islands between China and other claimant countries. China's position is clear and consistent: it has indisputable sovereignty over the South China Sea islands and their adjacent waters, but not the whole South China Sea.

Meanwhile, China seeks to maintain peace and stability in the South China Sea and calls for adherence to the principle of 'putting aside disputes and seeking joint development' in the region.

Myth Four: China threatens freedom of navigation and overflight in the South China Sea. The shipping lanes of the South China Sea are among the busiest in the world, and between 70 and 80 per cent of China's maritime transport of energy and goods passes through the region. Ensuring freedom of navigation and overflight in this region meets not only the requirement of international law but also China's fundamental interests. All countries have unimpeded access to normal navigation and flight activities in the South China Sea under international law, over which there is no disagreement.

China is also ready to offer other countries joint use of its facilities in the South China Sea for humanitarian rescue and disaster. In the same spirit, countries should act in accordance with international law when exercising freedom of navigation and overflight, and respect the sovereignty, security and relevant rights and interests of coastal states.

Myth Five: China intends to change the 'status quo' in the South China Sea. What exactly is this 'status quo'? Before 2013, the term rarely featured in diplomatic discussions on South China Sea disputes. Then came the US strategy of rebalancing the Asia-Pacific, and claimants in the disputed seas began to embrace the idea of defending the 'status quo'. It should be clear that China does not recognize the so-called status quo of the Philippines and other countries that are occupying China's islands and reefs through illegal means.

Myth Six: China is building 'artificial islands' in the South China Sea. The construction activities on China's islands and reefs are conducted on natural features over which China has sovereignty and which form part of the Nansha Islands. They are fundamentally different from the 'artificial islands, installations and structures' defined in the Law of the Sea.

Myth Seven: China's relevant islands and reefs are low-tide elevations with no territorial status. In accordance with international law, China's sovereignty over the Nansha Islands covers not only the islands itself, but also the islands, reefs, cays and sands that form the Nansha Islands and related waters. In 1935, 1947 and 1983, the Chinese government published the names of the South China Sea islands, including the collective and individual names of the Nansha Islands, including its components and various natural features. China's sovereignty over the Nansha Islands and its components has a full historical and legal basis.

Some countries have tried to separate the Nansha Islands from its components, willfully claiming that the related natural features have no territorial status. This is nothing but an out-of-context interpretation of international law.

Myth Eight: China is accelerating the militarization of the South China Sea. Since its rebalancing to the Asia-Pacific, the US has deepened its intervention in South China Sea disputes. To accuse China of militarizing the South China Sea is groundless. On the contrary, the

South China Sea is being militarized by high-profile displays of military strength and frequent and large-scale military drills by certain countries and their allies. China is committed to a path of peaceful development. This stance is consistent and clear-cut. The constructions in the South China Sea are mainly for civilian purposes, and with the acknowledged goal of better safeguarding China's territorial sovereignty and maritime rights and interests.

Myth Nine: China's construction activities damage the coral reefs and marine ecology. As the owner of the Nansha Islands, China cares more than any other country about the ecological preservation of the islands, reefs and the surrounding waters. Its construction activities place equal importance on environmental preservation.

Myth Ten: China is becoming assertive in the South China Sea. This seems to be the consensus in the media, academic journals and other professional venues. In fact, China's actions in the South China Sea are necessary to protect its legitimate interests and are justified reactions to provocations by other claimant states. Tensions in the region can be attributed to collusion between the US and regional claimant states. It is popularly believed that, without Washington's backing and high-profile policy of 'returning to Asia', regional states would not be so eager to challenge China's interests in the South China Sea.

China will continue to safeguard peace and stability in the South China Sea and promote the development of neighboring countries. Regardless of the result of the arbitration, China will continue to work closely with ASEAN countries to safeguard peace and stability and uphold freedom of navigation in the South China Sea, so as to eventually turn it into a 'sea of peace, friendship and cooperation'.

MAKING THE BRICS AN ENGINE OF THE NEW ROUND OF GLOBALIZATION

In the new round of globalization, the BRICS countries should take advantage of global trade and investment rules and institutions in order to enhance their positions in the global value chain, to promote and lead a strong, inclusive and sustainable growth in the global economy. Therefore, promoting trade and investment among the BRICS, strengthening rule-making and negotiating bargaining power should be at the core of the BRICS agenda.

In June 2017, the BRICS Forum on Political Parties, Think Tanks and Civil Society Organizations was held in Fuzhou, China. Thirty-seven political parties from 26 countries, more than 400 representatives from 105 think tanks and 79 civil society organizations attended the forum. Liu Yunshan, a member of the Standing Committee of the Political Bureau of the CPC Central Committee, attended the opening ceremony. Before the closing of the forum, Dr. Wang Wen read The Research Report on the BRICs and Globalization on behalf of the research team. This paper is a condensed version of the report.

ON THE OCCASION OF THE TENTH ANNIVERSARY OF THE BRICS MECHANISM, the BRICS Summit was held in India on the topic of efficiency, inclusiveness and common solutions. The BRICS countries, the G20, the United Nations and the Shanghai Cooperation Organization are the four strategic platforms for China's participation in global governance, and the BRICS countries are the most prominent and important platforms for China to exert its influence. The BRICS Summit held in China in 2017 will be China's most important event of 'home' diplomacy.

Global trade is shrinking, global economic recovery is fragile and uneven, protectionism is on the rise and anti-globalization developments, such as Brexit, are becoming increasingly serious. IMF President Christine Lagarde said earlier that the world economy was recovering slowly and that developing countries would contribute more than three quarters of global growth this year and next, making it a major contributor to world economic growth. Among the BRICS nations, both China and India continue to record high economic growth, while Brazil and Russia are showing signs of recovery. As the leader of developing economies, the prospects for economic growth in the BRICS countries are bright and the trend of future development can be expected.

BRICS's institutionalized mechanism is a force in global governance

In 2001, Jim O'Neill, then chief economist of Goldman Sachs, first introduced the concept of BRIC (Brazil, Russia, India and China). South Africa became a member of the BRICS at the Sanya Summit in 2011. By 2050, the BRIC countries will join the US and Japan as the world's six largest economies. Today, BRICS accounts for 43 of the world's population, with gold reserves and foreign exchange reserves accounting for 40 per cent of the world's total. The GDP of BRICS accounts for 21 per cent of the world's total, with the BRICS contributing more than 50 per cent to world economic growth over the past decade. While resource-based BRICS countries such as Russia, Brazil and South Africa have seen their growth decline as a result of the collapse in commodity prices, as a whole, BRICS' economic and investment performance remain relatively strong and they have huge growth potential, making it a bright spot in global economic growth.

The BRICS' accelerated institutional construct was triggered by the unprecedented financial crisis of 2008. In fact, the BRICS countries held their first meeting of foreign ministers as early as 2006. Two years later, in response to the financial crisis, the G20 meeting of central bank governors and finance ministers was upgraded to become the G20 Leaders' Summit, and the first BRICS heads of state summit was held in 2009. The common pursuit of global governance has accelerated the process of institutionalization of BRICS countries, which now has a comprehensive, multi-tiered and wide-ranging cooperative governance architecture. At the top is the BRICS summit of leaders, followed by issue-driven ministerial meetings, involving foreign ministers, high-level security representatives, finance ministers, central bankers, and trade, science and technology ministers. Senior officials and working groups will provide technical support to the ministerial meetings, such as the forum on state-owned enterprises, trade and economy, and the urbanization forum. There are also think tanks, business councils, friendly cities and local government forums and business forums dedicated to providing intellectual and information support.

The BRICS agreed at the Durban meeting in South Africa in 2013 to gradually develop the BRICS countries into a comprehensive mechanism for daily and long-term coordination on major global economic and political issues. With their economic and political rise, BRICS countries are playing an increasingly important role in global economic and political affairs. President Xi Jinping stressed that BRICS cooperation should be two-wheel drive: one political, the other economic; both an engine of the world's economy and a shield of international peace. Therefore, the development of BRICS economic and trade cooperation has gone beyond the general sense of mutual benefit, rising to the strategic height of deepening coordination and cooperation in various fields of international politics and the economy. Through this platform, BRICS nations can participate in negotiations on international economic and trade rules and the restructuring of the economic and trade system, and develop bilateral, multilateral and plurilateral economic and trade investment rules, with BRICS countries as the mainstay, as well as representing developing countries and emerging economies to formulate global economic, trade and investment rules. In addition, the platform can boost trade and investment within the BRICS and between the BRICS nations and the world. This will not only have an impact on global economic and trade investment, but will also lead to a new round of globalization.

China has grown into the largest trading partner and investor in Russia, Brazil, India and South Africa, and it has a larger economy and more trade than the other four countries combined. As the world's largest country in the global trade of goods, and the second largest in trade of services and foreign investment, China faces a daunting challenge in how it can play a central role in promoting economic, trade and investment cooperation among the BRICS countries, and how it can lead BRICS countries to integrate into global value chains and participate in global governance to reverse the sluggish world economy.

The BRICS are an engine of a new round of globalization.

The World Trade Organization and the United Nations Conference on Trade and Development (UNCTAD) predict a decline in international investment this year by 10-15 per cent. The IMF forecasts global economic growth of 3.1 per cent and trade growth of 2.8 per cent in 2016. Global trade growth will be below 3 per cent for the fifth year in a row. The 'Triffin dilemma' of the US dollar remains unresolved, with major world economies being seriously divided, plus the fact that the US economic recovery is sufficient to exit into the path of raising interest rates. Meanwhile, Europe and Japan are stepping up their quantitative easing monetary policies, but even after entering negative interest rates, their economies will have a hard time picking up.

In 2008, excessive financial liberalization led to the financial crisis, which in turn caused trade protectionism. This crisis-induced protectionism further restrained globalization, thus leading to a sharp decline in trade. With weak world economic recovery, a new round of globalization is urgently needed.

Given the rapid economic growth of developing countries, the world economic landscape has fundamentally changed. Developed countries accounted for 65.7 per cent of the world's GDP in 2008, but this fell to 45.7 per cent in 2013. In terms of trade and investment, developed countries' global imports fell from 50 per cent to 37 per cent. Almost 90 per cent of economic growth came from developing countries between 2008 and 2011. By 2030, emerging economies' share of global GDP is expected to rise from 38 per cent in 2008 to 63 per cent, while their share of global trade will exceed 40 per cent and they will contribute 70 per cent of the world's economic growth.

BRICS, which represents the interests of developing countries, is leading the wave of innovation, inclusiveness and sharing, and is becoming the engine of new globalization. The recently concluded G20 summit in Hangzhou put forward the idea of inclusive growth as the mainstay in the new round of globalization for the first time. The inclusiveness finds its best expression in the presence of a large number of developing countries, including the BRICS nations. It also integrates development issues into macro policy framework for the first time, implements the sustainable development agenda of 2030 and can help in the industrialization process in the least developed countries and Africa.

The BRICS face multiple challenges

Affected by the impact of the international financial crisis, global economic recovery is weak. The growth rate of the BRICS countries is slowing down, the negative spillover of the Fed rate increase and quantitative easing in Europe and Japan has also brought challenges to the BRICS countries whose economic development is not balanced. Talk of a BRICS collapse is also rife. Therefore, the BRICS urgently need to further strengthen cooperation in order to cope with the serious challenges that may affect their economic growth.

First of all, the similarity of the industrial structure of the BRICS countries can easily lead to a trade war. BRICS countries are all emerging economies, most of which are at the low end of the industrial chain and have low product technology content. From production structure, consumption structure to trade structure, even in the global industrial chain and value chain, their product positioning is similar, so it is easy to produce competition.

Second, some BRICS countries, affected by the financial crisis in Europe and the US as well as the European debt crisis, are facing hurdles on the path to economic growth. In particular, the economic growth rate of Brazil has fallen continuously as the risk of economic contraction increases with frequent changes in political regime. In Russia's case, given the commodities slump and EU and American sanctions, the government will have to fight an uphill battle to grow its economy that mainly relies on energy exports. South Africa also faces lower commodity prices and a downturn in its economy.

Finally, under multiple global regional trade agreements, the BRICS are also facing crowding-out effects. At present, there are 3,304 bilateral and multilateral economic and trade agreements in the world, and the fragmentation of rules has caused the 'spaghetti bowl effect'. Despite the problems of the TPP and TTIP, developed countries will not give up their dominant power in developing the international economic and trade rules. These regional agreements and economic and trade rules that are dominated by developed nations could still have a severe impact on the BRICS.

BRICS should jointly promote the 'Belt and Road' initiative

During the 2009-14 financial crisis, BRICS' total international trade managed to grow at an average annual rate of more than 30 per cent. At present, given the continuing low price of commodities such as energy and agricultural products, and minerals, the economic growth of the BRICS countries has been uneven. In 2015, Brazil, Russia, India, China and South Africa recorded GDP growth rates of -3.8 per cent, -3.7 per cent, 7.6 per cent, 6.9 per cent and 1.3 per cent respectively.

In contrast to the strong economic growth in China and India, the other BRICS economies are under greater downward pressure. Therefore, it is highly necessary to stimulate the BRICS economies by promoting and reinvigorating trade and investment between the BRICS.

Between January and August 2015, Brazil's investment in China rose by 48 per cent year-on-year, India's investment in China rose by 55 per cent and South Africa's investment in China grew by 91 per cent. Despite the fact that these statistics are based on a low investment base, it indicates that there are great investment opportunities within the BRICS. The BRICS are the most representative of emerging and booming markets, with more than US$336bn in trade between the BRICS countries in 2012. Bilateral trade between China and the other BRICS countries totaled more than US$300bn. The average growth rate of BRICS economies was more than twice that of developed economies. By 2020, BRICS economies will account 25 per cent of the world economy.

To maintain the economic development of the BRICS countries, it is necessary to strengthen the partnership among the five countries, enhance internal coordination, enable trade and investment to drive economic growth, and promote the optimization and upgrading of the BRICS structural adjustment. First of all, the BRICS countries should not only carry out policy communication and coordination through platforms such as G20 and APEC-UNCTAD, but also make full use of the BRICS platform to facilitate trade and investment rule-making and other negotiations, thus leading a new round of globalization. As an important platform for trade and investment, BRICS countries best represent the interests of developing countries and emerging economies. In 2014, the BRICS countries adopted the 'Action Plan on Investment and Trade Facilitation' through the BRICS, and 'The BRICS Framework for Cooperation in Trade and Investment' and the BRICS views on international investment agreements have been implemented to strengthen cooperation in infrastructure, finance and other areas among BRICS countries. Second, the BRICs countries should take the lead in implementing the G20 trade growth strategy and the guiding principles of global investment. In 2017, the G20 Hangzhou Summit adopted the first G20 Global Trade Growth Strategy and the G20 Global Investment Guidelines. BRICS countries, as G20 member states, should actively implement these trade growth strategies and investment guidelines, and drive G20 and global economic and trade investment growth.

Finally, the BRICS are located along the Belt and Road route, and the rapid growth of India's economy in recent years has brought new opportunities for BRICS' trade and investment. Russia's cooperation with the Belt and Road initiative on the Eurasian Economic Union also presents important cooperation opportunities for economic and trade investment. South Africa and Brazil are rich in mineral resources. With the development of the Belt and Road initiative, the demand for resources for infrastructure construction will increase, so there will also be many economic and trade investment opportunities.

Therefore, the BRICS countries should strengthen economic and trade investment cooperation, jointly promote the Belt and Road construct, improve their economic development plans and work together to promote economic integration with China's Belt and Road programs.

Developing a nation's manufacturing industry is the foundation of economic growth. Most BRICS countries are rich in resources, with obvious advantages in human resources and technology. By coordinating the development of strategies and rules for the growth of investment trade and jointly promoting the Belt and Road construction, it will help promote economic and trade exchanges among the BRICS countries and facilitate BRICS' integration into global industrial chains, promote exports of high value-added products, upgrade their position in global value chains and effectively enhance the international competitiveness of BRICS countries as a whole.

BRICS should work together to lead a new round of globalization

The core of the current round of globalization is the new industry represented by the digital economy, the symbol of which is the rise of developing countries. The 2008 financial crisis severely impacted developed countries in Europe and America. The G20's global governance architecture, replacing the G7 that was made up of developed countries, has played an important role in fighting the financial crisis to save the world economy. The summit of BRICS leaders, which began in 2009, also plays a pivotal role in the new round of globalization, acting as the engine of world economic growth. In the new round of globalization, the BRICS countries need to take advantage of the rules and institutions of global trade and investment, because it can enhance its position in the global value chain and enable the global economy to grow in a strong, inclusive and sustainable fashion. Therefore, promoting trade and investment among the BRICS and strengthening rule-making and negotiation capacity should be made top priority on the BRICS agenda. The BRICS countries should make full use of this platform, strengthen trade and investment facilitation, and reduce barriers to trade and investment, provide financial support for infrastructure development, boost growth in BRICS and global trade and investment, and restart the engines of growth in trade and investment.

In the spring of 2017, Wang Wen made a keynote speech at the BRICS national think-tank symposium on The Future of the BRICS

The current global infrastructure funding gap is huge, and the World Bank and similar institutions can only provide US$300bn, which is far short of meeting global financial needs, especially in developing countries. To this end, the BRICS Leaders' Summit in 2012 proposed the establishment of the BRICS New Development Bank. In 2014, the BRICS Leaders' Summit in Brazil signed an agreement establishing the BRICS New Development Bank (NDB) and the Treaty on Establishing the BRIC Emergency Reserve Arrangement. In 2015, the NDB announced its opening and went into operation. In addition to providing development finance, the BRICS have also set up a US$100bn contingency reserve arrangement to help BRICS countries cope with liquidity pressures and strengthen financial stability.

The NDB and the contingent reserve arrangement (CRA) not only support the real economic growth of developing countries and provide important public goods for the new round of globalization, but also promote the economic integration of BRICS countries. This is a financial safety net for the BRICS.

In 2013, the US signed an agreement with the central banks of the Eurozone, the UK, Japan, Canada and Switzerland to solidify the original bilateral currency swap network, BSAs, into an unlimited, indefinite period. This is actually a shield for developed countries from future financial crisis and something that will enhance financial stability. Both the NDB and CRA help to provide financial support and strengthen financial stability for BRICS and other developing countries. While improving the international financial governance system, we should promote the reform of the international financial system, including the share of the IMF and the World Bank. The typical feature of the new round of globalization is based on the development of new sectors such as wireless networks and intelligence. Therefore, it is necessary to innovate new modes of economic growth and establish new economic and trade and investment rules.

For the BRICs countries to give better leadership in this new round of globalization, they should, first of all, strengthen structural reform and promote innovative growth through economic restructuring and optimization and upgrading. Just as China has implemented structural reform of the supply side for the new economic normal, we must achieve what we call 'three to go, one reduction and one subsidy' in order to speed up structural reform of the supply side, and persist in innovation, coordination, environmental awareness, openness and the concept of shared development. Likewise, in order to achieve a new round of globalization, BRICS countries also need structural reform, innovation and growth.

BRICS countries should firmly support the WTO multilateral trading system, implement the Agreement on Trade Facilitation of the WTO, promote negotiations on economic and trade investment rules, including electronic commerce, and actively implement the BRICS economic partnership strategy. This is necessary in order to realize the blueprint for BRICS economic and trade cooperation, that is, to press ahead with the BRICS countries to build 'integrated markets', multi-level circulation, land, sea and air links and cultural exchanges, in order to promote economic, trade and investment among nations.

To this end, it is necessary to accelerate the implementation of the BRICS economic partnership strategy. With structural adjustment and innovative growth, we should also promote intra-industry trade among the BRICS, benefit-sharing among BRICS countries and BRICS mega-markets, thus driving emerging economies into global value chains, leading a new round of globalization. In addition, we should deepen financial cooperation among the BRICS countries, take advantage of the opportunity of the renminbi joining the Special Drawing Right to become a world currency, enhance the scale of currency swaps among the BRICS countries, strengthen their financial capacity and support the use of the renminbi in BRICS countries. Simultaneously, BRICS countries should make full use of new development banks and emergency reserve arrangements to increase financial support for trade financing, to strengthen infrastructure connectivity as well as international financial cooperation, and to strengthen the financial governance capacity and voice of BRICS countries.

Finally, BRICS countries should take the leading role in developing rules in the upcoming round of globalization. The BRICS trade ministers' meeting will be held before the summit. In 2011, China initiated the establishment of the BRICS Economic and Trade Ministers' Meeting Mechanism. So far, it has convened five meetings and adopted several cooperation plans, such as the BRICS Framework for Cooperation in Trade and Investment and the BRICS Economic Partnership Strategy.

The BRICS are planning a free trade zone and jointly building the Belt and Road, facilitating the economic integration process, as well as leading a new round of globalization. At the same time, BRICS will also give play to the comparative advantages of India, Brazil, Russia and China in trade in services and goods. Against the backdrop of a new round of globalization, the BRICS are pushing for economic and trade rules that are in the interest of developing countries and emerging economies with which BRICS countries can lead the global economy to sustained growth.

Liu Ying co-authored this report. Chinese, English, Portuguese and Russian editions of The BRICS Countries: The Engine of New Globalization were published by the New World Press in August 2017.

III

THE WORLD NEEDS TO REASSESS CHINA'S CONTRIBUTIONS

THE WORLD GREATLY UNDERESTIMATES CHINA'S CONTRIBUTION

Some people have claimed that China's current economic slowdown threatens the growth of the world economy. I think this assessment is unfair. In the past, when we had more than 10 per cent growth, many accused China of polluting the environment with excessive emissions. Now, our growth rate has fallen but the environment is improving and the quality of growth is improving, yet many are still critical of China. If the world was wrong in underestimating China's growth in the past, they are making a similar mistake in underestimating China's contribution to global governance.

The G20 Summit's Pre-Summit and the G20 Think Tank Summit were held from November 13 to 15, 2015, in Antalya, Turkey. More than 400 politicians, think tank scholars and representatives of international organizations from more than 20 countries participated. As a representative of China's think tank community, Dr. Wang Wen was invited to deliver a keynote speech entitled 'Prospects for the upcoming G20 Summit in China' at the closing ceremony of the summit on the morning of November 15

THANK YOU AGAIN FOR THIS INVITATION AND FOR GIVING ME THE opportunity to share with you my thoughts on the prospect of the upcoming G20 to be hosted by China. I feel humbled, as I must say that I can't hold out that prospect with 100 per cent accuracy, because the world is in a state of high uncertainty, just as the terror attack in Paris is shaping the G20 agenda. Perhaps something unexpected will happen in China in the next 10 months. Of course, I don't want bad things to happen, but something good to happen in an unexpected way.

On November 11, for example, China's e-commerce sector witnessed a shopping frenzy. An online store known as Tmall broke through the Rmb100bn transaction barrier in just 12 minutes, or US$15.7bn. It is important to stress here that the 'double 11' shopping spree did not just involve Chinese consumers, but consumers from more than 180 countries around the world who shopped simultaneously on various Chinese e-commerce sites. This demonstrates the integration of the global economy and shows how China contributes to global growth and what new impetus it can bring to global growth.

So what contribution does China make to the world? Let me share with you some statistics.

- The contribution of China's economic growth to the global economy. In 2008-14, China alone contributed more than 30 per cent of the world's 'new economy', averaging 44 per cent in the last three years. Even at 7 per cent, China's economy is now growing at an annual rate of US$800bn, surpassing the double-digit pace of growth before the financial crisis. It has made a great contribution to stabilizing global growth.
- The contribution of China's financial stability to the world. Since 2008, China has experienced no major financial volatility. In 2014, the weighted average interest rates for interbank lending and bond buybacks were 3.48 per cent and 3.49 per cent, respectively. Non-financial companies have a weighted average interest rate of 6.77 per cent, within a stable and reasonable range, thus constituting a strong stabilizer for a global environment characterized by 'big deflation'.
- China's foreign investment promotes global growth. China's

foreign direct investment is expected to exceed US$1tn for the first time in 2015. By 2020, China will invest more than US$5tn.
- China has made a great contribution to the sustainable development of the world's economy. It has lifted a cumulative total of 600m people out of poverty over the past 30 years in accordance with the UN standards for poverty eradication, accounting for 90 per cent of the total number of people taken out of poverty in the world during this period.

Some critics have argued that China's current economic slowdown threatens the growth of the world economy. I think this assessment is unfair. In the past, when we had more than 10 per cent growth, many accused China of polluting the environment with excessive harmful emissions; now that our growth is down and the environment and quality of growth are improving, there are many who are still critical of China. I hope that the world will come to have a fairer assessment of China.

If the world has underestimated China's growth in the past, it is now downplaying China's contribution to global governance. Yet these contributions are what prompt China to host the G20 Summit. So, you must be interested in knowing about the rationale behind China's bid to host the 2016 summit. Now, permit me to share with you the four key words.

The first is hope. China has not waged or participated in any war over the past 30 years. It has not produced any refugees or bombed any other countries. China is a peace-loving global power. It is participating in a growing number of global governance mechanisms that allow the world to see the dynamism and momentum of further growth. China is actively involved in the G20, BRICS and APEC mechanisms. In fact, China has signed 14 free trade agreements with 22 countries through the establishment of a global network of free trade zones. China's involvement in the rescue plan following the financial crisis in the US and Eurozone, and the establishment of the Asian Infrastructure Investment Bank (AIIB), have attracted the participation of more than 50 countries, making up for a shortfall in infrastructure investment in the

Asia-Pacific region. The role that China plays testifies to the vitality of a responsible power, allowing people to see the hope of the world.

The second is innovation. Innovation is one of the biggest features championed by the current Chinese administration. China is encouraging all enterprises and individuals to invest in and confirm the protection of intellectual property rights; to incentivize innovative business models in the promotion of new technologies; and to facilitate the commercialization of new technologies. China's innovation will help build a 'global innovation system' that will give a fundamental impetus to sustainable global economic growth.

The third is connectivity. China now has the world's largest total trade volume, its economic size has reached second place in the world and the scale of its actual utilization of foreign capital topped the world ranking for the first time in 2014. That year, outward foreign direct investment stood at US$123.12bn, ranking third in the world. By 2020, China is expected to become the world's largest economy, and the proportion of import and export trade and two-way global capital flows will rise further. Now China is promoting the Belt and Road initiative, the purpose of which is to provide public goods for the international community once its national strength has increased, and to promote the orderly and free flow of economic elements, the efficient allocation of resources and the deep integration of the market, to coordinate economic policies among countries along the route, to carry out regional cooperation on a larger scale, at a higher level and at a deeper level, and to work together to create an open, inclusive, balanced framework for regional economic cooperation. It is not only the trend of the times, but also the driving force of China's economic growth.

The fourth word is inclusiveness. China has just published its 13th five-year plan, which will decide the country's development policy in the next five years. This is the first time that Chinese economists have drawn up a five-year plan by taking into consideration the global economic situation. One of the major strategies is to work together to build Belt and Road to connect the continents of Asia, Europe, Africa and nearby seas. We should establish and strengthen partnership among those countries along the project, build a comprehensive, multi-level and complex network of connectivity, and realize the diversified, autonomous, balanced, sustainable development and international cooperation in production capacity of Belt and Road countries. The Belt and Road connectivity project will facilitate the interface and coupling of development strategies of countries along the route, tap the potential of intraregional markets, promote investment and consumption, and create demand and employment. We will enhance people-to-people exchanges in all countries along the Belt and Road so that people from different nations can meet, respect each other, and live in harmony and prosperity. To sum up, China is now proposing the concept of a 'community of shared future', and I hope that this concept can become a fundamental value of the G20. In particular, a myriad of non-traditional security issues are emerging that pose a severe challenge to the international order and the survival of mankind. Therefore, no matter where we live or what religion we believe, we share one thing in common – we live in a community of shared destiny. As the primary platform of global governance, we should nurture the consciousness of a community of shared human destiny and face the complex situation and global issues pertaining to the world economy.

This is my understanding of why China is so committed to hosting 2016 G20 Summit.

THE US SHOULD LEARN FROM CHINA IN UNDERTAKING SOME POLITICAL REFORM

The American intellectual community should not speculate on when China will collapse, but instead recognize China's political progress, and learn from each other and respect each other so that both countries can unite to address global challenges.

On May 6-7, 2015, the World Forum on Chinese Studies, jointly sponsored by the Shanghai Academy of Social Sciences and the Carter Center, was held in the US state of Atlanta. At the opening ceremony and dinner reception on May 6, former Chinese Foreign Minister Li Zhaoxing, and Cui Yuying, vice minister of publicity of the CPC Central Committee and deputy director of the Information Office of the State Council, made separate remarks. This paper is a translation of Wang Wen's keynote speech entitled 'Think tanks, media and the new process of democratization in China'.

Forgive me for not having begun with honorifics, such as 'Ladies and Gentlemen', because almost all of you present here today are among the most influential scholars of political science and international relations in both China and the United States. Most of the scholars are senior; some in fact, have taught me before. As a junior scholar, I feel privileged to be able to participate in such an important forum on an equal footing with the teachers. I am now executive director of a new think tank called the Chongyang Institute for Financial Studies, Renmin University of China. I used to work for a newspaper agency for nearly eight years as an editorial director and editorial drafter. More than two years ago, I was a co-founder of the Chongyang Institute for Financial Studies. Over the past few months, I have been interviewed on numerous occasions, and the most frequently asked question is why it has taken only two years for Chongyang to rank among the top 10 think tanks at home and abroad.

Of course, ranking doesn't mean everything, and I don't want to continue advertising for my institute. I think what I am driving at is that Chongyang has always been strong in communicating ideas, which is related to my past work experience. I remember that I received an important phone call about six months after our institute went into operation. I was told that President Xi Jinping read one of my articles circulated in the media. Of course, I was very excited. After that, I continued to get a lot of feedback from important government officials. I say this because I want to emphasize that think tanks and the media can combine their effort to push for a more democratic and scientific decision-making mechanism. Over the past two years, President Xi has repeatedly stressed the importance of think tanks in public and invited scholars from think tanks to lecture more to the Chinese leadership in the Zhongnanhai compound and to discuss state matters. This administration proves to be much better at using and adopting advice from professional policy researchers than ever before. To this end, China has set up about 200 new think tanks, or converted research institutions into think tanks, over the past two years. Think tanks have become a force for democratization, and that force is going to grow stronger. This's the first point I want to make.

Second, changes in the media. China began to enter the Internet 2.0

era in 2009. 'Internet 2.0' refers to the emergence of many interactive web tools. For example, Weibo, which is a Twitter upgrade in China, has become an important driving force of information dissemination and political democratization in China. For many years, it has been a popular tool for anti-corruption campaigns. In 2013, China entered the WeChat era. WeChat is more immersive and more elite than Weibo. At present, WeChat has more than 500m users, including most of China's elite. They form WeChat groups, exchange ideas, spread information and then aggregate public opinion so that the nation's senior leadership can access and listen to public opinion. The way public opinion is conveyed to high-level government officials is more convenient, more efficient and clearer. If Weibo is a bottom-to-top power of political checks and balances, WeChat is more like a channel of political transmission between the top and the bottom. In the era of WeChat, the gap between Chinese decision-makers and public opinion has narrowed and more barriers have been eliminated, and the theory of six-dimensional social relations has become invalid in WeChat space.

It is often found that useful buzzwords that feature prominently on the internet will be used in public speeches by President Xi Jinping and other state leaders, indicating that policymakers touch base with the existing social situation. At the same time, the state media tend to rely on networking, and the government has become more skilled in the use of social media. The website of *People's Daily*, thepeoples.net, has seen its share price rise several times in three years. The enormous influence of the official Wechatting, such as the Learning Group, has shaped public opinion in an all-round fashion.

Looking around the world, riots and political unrest have occurred in many countries, but in China, the Communist Party of China under Xi Jinping is currently at its highest level of support since 1978. This is partly because the CPC has adapted to the internet era of political governance.

Third, the wealthy elite has become a strong force to support social stability and development, as well as one for national economic expansion. At present, Chinese society is setting off the largest-ever innovation campaign. In Beijing, Shanghai, Guangzhou and Shenzhen, there are tens of thousands of company start-up cafes and innovative incubators. Tens of thousands of new billionaires have emerged during this period of 'innovation fever', and they are mostly young people born in the 1980s and 1990s. This new phenomenon came into being partly because the Chinese government encourages innovation, and partly because of the role model set by the new generations of self-made billionaires. Today, Alibaba's Jack Ma Yun, Xiaomi's Lei Jun and many new wealthy upstarts are the objects of emulation by China's younger generation. They are also contributing to the changing landscape of the Chinese zeitgeist. At present, the 'eight provisions' based on the precept of incorruptibility and simplification of government affairs are enjoying tremendous popular support among the general public. *Running Man* is a TV show that features togetherness and wholesomeness, and it is becoming one of the highest-rated entertainment shows in China. Various indicators show that the Chinese zeitgeist is at its highest point since reform and opening up began in the late 1970s, which I call the political 'new normal'.

With regard to the above three points, I would like to make the following three conclusions:

First, there are three forces in parallel with political power: the power of knowledge, society and wealth. In Xi Jinping's time, there is a convergence of objectives and directions that the three major forces and political power strive for. Therefore, a huge political consensus is reached to promote socio-political progress, the great rejuvenation of the Chinese nation and the realization of Chinese Dream, and so on.

Second, America's understanding of China's political reform is still out of touch with the reality of China's political development. Professor David Shambaugh's 'China collapse theory' that he pronounced in early March is only a reflection of this disconnection. More important, the American political engagement with China has never been free from the influence of 'American-style doctrine', that is, the US as a model and benchmark of global political development. It is a very simplistic way to measure the progress of Chinese political development. Unfortunately only two options are available: China is either democratic or undemocratic.

In other words, even if the ideas of Francis Fukuyama, author of *The End of History,* have been discredited, the end of history theory continues to exist. Mainstream American society is still proud of its own political system and maintains a long-term sense of moral superiority over the political development of other countries.

Third, there are of course many problems with China's political system. In the American political system, there are many things that China can learn from. These include attracting foreign talent, political communication and the revolving door mechanism. But I also hope that the US can see the advantages of China's political system. Of course, Chinese political institutions also face huge challenges: corruption, declining economic growth, environmental pollution and so on, and I agree that it is even harder to carry out reform than it was at the beginning of 1990s. But on the whole, I maintain that China's political development is still conducive to the current social transformation and continuing development of the country. As I argued in a 2014 article entitled 'The collapse of China's collapse theory', the American intellectual community should no longer speculate on when China will collapse, but instead recognize China's political progress, learn from each other and respect each other so that China and the US can work together to meet global challenges.

Wang Wen at the Peterson Institute for International Economics in Washington DC, September 16, 2015

Finally, I want to say: believe in China. China's future will be better.

Q: Several speakers have just talked about anti-corruption. We all agree that China's current corruption is serious and has much to do with its institutional mechanism. China must carry out institutional reform in order to get rid of corruption. What do you think?

Wang Wen: I am an economist now. I am reluctant to comment on political issues. And because of the time constraint, I will only respond to the question with three observations. First, anti-corruption is a consensus in Chinese society, where no one has the guts to oppose it publicly. President Xi Jinping's determination to fight corruption is also very firm. According to President Xi, the fight against corruption is a new, yet daunting historical task. His anti-corruption campaign has yielded great results and surely he will carry it on. Second, there are institutional reasons for fighting corruption, but Western democracy is not a cure for corruption. India and Nigeria are 'democratic' countries, but corruption is much worse there than in China. The US in early 20th century was a 'democracy', but corruption was still running rampant. Third, I believe that democracy is mainly related to the stages of social development. At present, China's per capita GDP is about US$6,000. I believe that in 10 or 20 years, the issue of corruption will surely be brought under control when China's per capita GDP reaches US$10,000 to US$20,000.

Q: I come from Hong Kong and I'm a regular commentator on Hong Kong TV. But even in Hong Kong, there is no absolute freedom of speech. You talked about media freedom in China just now, but China still does not have the freedom to criticize the status quo. What do you think of this?

Wang Wen: I think otherwise. To me, China does have freedom to criticize. For instance, Chinese social media sites offer considerable space for public criticism. In fact, almost anything can be subject to public criticism. Even *People's Daily*, the mouthpiece of the CPC Central Committee, often publishes articles critical of the status quo. However, there is a bottom line in terms of free speech in every country. Even in the US, not everything can be said publicly. Political correctness is an absolute must. Therefore, the issue of criticism in the Chinese media is not at all whether we can be critical, but rather how to criticize. Of course, China is in the transitional period where the red line of free speech is still evolving.

UNDERSTANDING THE CHINESE VIEW OF CLIMATE FINANCE

China is a big country with determination and responsibility. In my opinion, China is undergoing a green revolution, but it still needs to work with the world. Therefore, the world should encourage China more, and have a greater appreciation of its response to climate change and the challenge it faces in climate finance, rather than blindly criticizing it for polluting the environment.

From May 20 to 22, 2015, the Climate Finance Conference was held in Paris, France, at the headquarters of the United Nations Educational, Scientific and Cultural Organization (UNESCO). The topic of the conference on the last day was entitled 'Climate Finance Day – Paris 2015'. More than 1,300 representatives from Europe, the US, Japan, India and other major countries attended the meeting. France's Minister of Finance and Public Finance, Michel Sabin, and the Minister of Foreign Affairs, Laurent Fabius, made the opening and closing remarks, respectively. Dr. Wang Wen was the only Chinese participant invited to this meeting and he explained China's position and views in his speech. This paper is based on a translation of the recording of his speech.

I AM GRATEFUL TO THE ORGANIZER FOR THIS INVITATION AND FEEL HONORED to be the only Chinese speaker at such an important meeting. Perhaps I am also the only Chinese participant present on this occasion. China is the most populous country in the world but today, on Climate Finance Day, I feel rather lonely [laughter]. I wonder why the organizers didn't invite more Chinese participants. There are plenty out shopping on the streets of Paris! [laughter]

Why do I feel lonely at this time? Because climate finance, broadly speaking, happens to be a new term in the Chinese lexicon. I say this because just this past month the Chinese Finance Society's Green Finance Professional Committee was founded, the first official academic organization to tackle green finance in China. I have the privilege of being elected secretary-general of this organization. But frankly, even though I'm the secretary-general of Green Finance with a permanent teaching position at a renowned university, I have to admit that most Chinese don't understand the phrases 'green finance' or 'climate finance'.

So, the first point I want to address is a call to all trained experts in climate finance and green finance here today to go to China and tell the Chinese about the benefits of climate finance for the world and all of humanity, and what the benefits are for China. If 1.3bn people support climate finance, it is bound to run more smoothly around the world.

In April, in collaboration with the United Nations Environment Program (UNEP), we completed a monograph on the establishment of China's green financial system, which offers 14 green financial recommendations to the Chinese government. These include green banks, green loans, green bonds and environmental liability. But that's not enough. Europe can be a professor of climate finance and needs to share more knowledge with China.

Second, I would like to talk about low-carbon finance, or the status quo of climate finance in China. In 2008, China established the first environmental exchange. In 2010, the first energy conservation and emission reduction transaction was completed. However, China's low-carbon capital system is not yet mature, and the uncertainty of risk has dampened investors' enthusiasm in low-carbon finance. Therefore, we need help from developed countries in Europe and the US, and strengthened cooperation between China and developed countries that are doing well in low-carbon finance. We can jointly conduct training and seminars in the field of climate finance. We can also work together within the framework of G20. In return, Europe perhaps needs to listen more to the voices from China. Chongyang Institute for Financial Studies, Renmin University of China, is an important Chinese think tank dedicated to the study of G20. It is our sincere hope to work with you all.

Third, I want to share with you the Chinese concept of development. Now, speaking in Paris on China as a developing country, I understand you may not believe what I said regarding the many wealthy Chinese who are shopping outside on the streets. They buy perfume and bags as if they were choosing vegetables in their local grocery store. But to tell you the truth, this wealthy elite only make up 1 per cent of China's total population, or perhaps just 0.1 per cent. China is still a developing country, and it still has many poor people. So what China has to do now is to balance development with low carbon; we want both development and a low-carbon economy. This is no easy job for a large manufacturing country such as China, but we have been working on it. Europe needs to understand the challenge China faces.

I have sufficient data to prove this. China was one of the first countries to join the Kyoto Protocol and has long recognized that combating climate change is an international obligation and domestic responsibility. In 2014, China's carbon intensity was 33.8 per cent lower than in 2005. By 2020, China aims to reduce its gross domestic product per unit of carbon dioxide by 40-50 per cent compared with 2005. China is a big country with determination and responsibility. In my opinion, China is undergoing a green revolution, but it still needs the help of the whole world. With so many international media representatives here today, I would like to suggest that, instead of going to great lengths to criticize China for polluting the environment, you encourage China, understand the uphill battle it is fighting against climate change, and understand the challenge China is facing in the area of climate finance.

Q: What are China's specific policies related to green finance and what is its national strategy for green finance?

Wang Wen: China has done quite a lot to protect the environment. But according to many European media reports, it has done little more than pollute the environment. It is important to know that the Chinese are also human, and China has 1.3bn men and women, 20 times the size of the French population. They eat, drink, sleep, do business and are actively engaged in protecting the environment. They aspire to a better life and are looking forward to a brighter future. If you want me to elaborate on China's green finance policies, perhaps I will be the only one speaker on the floor today. [Laughter] Let me give you an example. Every five years, China draws up a five-year economic development plan. In 2016, it will issue the 13th five-year plan. Now it is clear that green finance will be written as an important component in the 13th five-year plan of financial reform and development. It is China's national policy on green finance and climate finance. Although the general public isn't well aware of it, the government has provided financial services through loans, private equity funds, bonds, shares, insurance, etc. Therefore, a series of specific policy and institutional arrangements have been made to channel social funds and public resources to environmentally friendly projects. The rationale behind all these efforts is that blue skies and white clouds, plus clear water and green mountains, should be an indispensable part of a better life for the Chinese people.

Q: Civil society is of great significance in shaping a country's climate policy. How do you view the relationship between civil society, public opinion and national climate finance?

Wang Wen: That's a very important question. As I said just now, the general public in China needs to have a better understanding of climate finance policies. Today, I've been listening very attentively and studying the views of many climate finance experts and political figures. I find that many Europeans are beginning to talk about the risks and risk prevention of 'climate finance'. However, the Chinese may not even know what climate finance means. We are clearly in different stages of development with regard to this issue. I took a stroll in Berlin three days ago and on the streets of Paris just yesterday, when I found that many Europeans are starting once again to ride bicycles. You know, in China, many of us have given up the bicycle and are beginning to enjoy the convenience of cars. Yet at least 70 per cent of Chinese have never driven a car, which is a rather complicated stage of development. Chinese policymakers must take into account the feelings of the general public and, of course, the concerns of all mankind about climate change. It is no easy job to strike a balance, so developed countries need to understand how hard the Chinese people have worked to resolve the issue.

THE CHINA AND AFRICA DEVELOPMENT PATHS SHOULD NOT BE CONFINED TO THE WESTERN MODEL

———

To pursue our national development, China and South Africa should not blindly copy the development models of other countries. Instead, we should rely on our own wisdom to cope with the challenges in the course of development and find a new path with our own characteristics. This is the process in which we, the intellectuals and think tank scholars from our two respective countries, can contribute.

From September 9 to 10, 2015, the Fourth China-Africa Think Tank Forum was held in Tshwane, South Africa. Renowned think tank scholars from both China and South Africa participated in the two-day discussion. Dr. Wang Wen was invited to deliver the keynote speech at the opening plenary meeting.

THANK YOU FOR INVITING ME TO ATTEND THE CHINA-AFRICA THINK TANK Forum. I consider this a learning opportunity, and one that allows me to travel to South Africa for the first time in my life. I am getting a real feeling for the charm of the Rainbow Nation.

Chinese President Xi Jinping has attached great importance to building Chinese think tanks. In 2013, the decision to 'strengthen the construction of new think tanks with Chinese characteristics' was written into the directive of the third plenary session of the 18th CPC Central Committee. This is the first time in history that 'think tank construction' has been written into documents of the Central Committee of the CPC, meaning that the development of think tanks is a top priority in China's national development strategy. There are now about 2,000 think tanks in China, many of which have been founded in recent years. It can be said that the best time for Chinese think tanks has arrived.

Chongyang Institute for Financial Studies, Renmin University of China, is a product of this think tank boom. Chongyang is currently regarded as one of the best among the many new-type think tanks in China. We were founded in early 2013, but because of our influential research output on global governance, especially on issues such as the G20, the Belt and Road initiative and outbound investment, Chongyang featured in the top 150 Global Think Tanks in the most recognized 2014 Global Think Tank Report released by the University of Pennsylvania. So far, only seven Chinese think tanks have been selected. We are also considered the youngest but fastest-growing Chinese think tank in history. Perhaps that is why I am honored to be able to deliver a keynote address at such an important forum and share with you some of our viewpoints.

About seven years ago, there was a heated debate among Chinese academics about whether China and South Africa should be compared. The debate involved scholars and researchers affiliated with Tsinghua University, Peking University, the Chinese Academy of Social Sciences, Renmin [the People's] University of China and other first-class education and research institutions in China. The comparison between China and South Africa, which was conducted from the perspective of 'human rights and labor costs', has for the first time sparked a broad interest in the new South Africa on the part of a significant number of China's intellectual elite.

Unfortunately, the debate was confined to the academic community; trained experts from think tanks in our respective countries were not involved. I hope that the current China-Africa Think Tank Forum will once again spark more intellectual exchange and comparison between the two countries.

In my opinion, there are at least three similarities between China and South Africa, each of which provides a strategic basis for cooperation between our respective think tanks.

In terms of stage of development, both China and South Africa are in a difficult period of transition. Over the past 20 years, South Africa managed to make the transition from apartheid to democracy. But at present, I understand that the intellectual circle in South Africa is debating how to improve the competence of national governance against the background of the transition to a democratic system, and how to solve the problems that arise during the second transition in terms of social development and economic expansion. In our case, after completing the first round of economic reforms and opening up, China is faced with the second transformation, namely industrial upgrading, improving quality and efficiency, and ecological protection. Therefore, the think tank communities of the two countries can conduct frequent discussions, share experiences, and encourage each other and boost mutual confidence.

From the point of view of regional contribution, China and South Africa are a mainstay of development in their respective regions, and they are both building what we call 'a community of shared destiny' that is designed to orient toward the future. As early as the end of 20th century, South Africa had conceived a strategic vision for 'Africa's rejuvenation' and launched a special African recovery fund and international aid agency, as well as a '2063 plan'. For a long time, South Africa's influence has been widely felt, and it has played a leadership role in Africa's development. It is also a member of the BRICS, G20 and, for several terms in a row, has been a non-permanent member of the UN Security Council. Its global influence is increasing dramatically. Therefore, think tanks in the two countries can carry out strategic cooperation and exchange ideas on the theme of 'regional rejuvenation' and expand and consolidate cooperation within the framework of the G20 and the BRICS mechanism.

In terms of financial strength, both China and South Africa are large entities, yet we face the daunting task of how to transform ourselves into financial powers. South Africa has the most developed financial system in Africa, with its insurance industry ranking sixth in the world and the Johannesburg Stock Exchange ranked eighth globally. But South Africa's financial system is heavily influenced by the European and American systems, and the rand exchange rate is not stable. Perhaps, 'big yet weak' is the current predicament of the financial industry in South Africa. China's financial sector is also in the middle of profound development. It has the world's largest bank assets and internet finance markets, but 'financial repression' has long restricted the improvement of China's financial efficiency. The two countries' financial think tanks can find many areas of cooperation in the field of finance.

Therefore, there is great room for extensive cooperation between China and South Africa, especially when it comes to upgrading overall strategic cooperation between China and Africa through South Africa. In this regard, I have the following three specific suggestions, with which I hope to further promote China's cooperation with Africa, especially with South Africa, through a think tank platform.

First, we should build upon the current China-Africa Think Tank Forum and expand it into the 'Alliance of China-Africa Think Tanks'. We should also build big data about the research projects of China-Africa think tanks, and share our research results with each other, strengthen mutual understanding of the Chinese and African intellectual communities and bridge the gap between China and Africa through intellectual exchange and decision-making consultation. Now that Zhejiang Normal University is widely considered one of the most important Africa research centers in China, Chongyang at Renmin University of China is also willing to participate and contribute our bit to the new establishment.

Second, through China-Africa think tank cooperation, we will seek to dock the Belt and Road initiative with the Africa Renaissance initiative, especially to explore business opportunities that match development projects with investment ones. The US$40bn Silk Road Fund has been put into operation, the BRICS New Development Bank has been set up and the Asian Infrastructure Investment Bank is about to be officially launched. Three new financial institutions will reshape the international financial structure. The two sides may use think tanks as a platform to further promote research and cooperation in the fields of currency exchange, trade settlement, financial supervision, risk prevention and so on, as well as a large number of trade-related investment projects.

For example, Yiwu, a city in Zhejiang province whose mayor is present here today, boasts the world's largest commodity distribution center. There are numerous trade and investment opportunities that Africa can avail of itself.

Third, through the cooperation of China-Africa think tanks, China will further enhance the global influence of the two countries. In 2016, China will host the G20 Summit. This is the first time in the G20's history that China will host a summit in which it is in charge of the top-level design of global governance. The Chongyang Institute for Financial Studies, Renmin University of China, is an important G20 research think tank and is willing to invite more South African think tanks to participate. In fact, Chongyang has hosted three G20 think tank summits in the past, all of which involved our South African counterparts. Hosting the G20 Summit is an important symbol of a country's global power status, and I suggest that South Africa considers hosting one itself, and Chongyang is ready to share its experience. If successful, it will be another year of power and glory after South Africa successfully hosted the FIFA World Cup in 2010.

To sum up, South Africa is a country worthy of global respect. South Africa's late president, Nelson Mandela, one of the most respected foreign leaders among the Chinese people, advocated a spirit of tolerance and reconciliation that defuses the century-old racial tensions that have plagued South Africa. His heroism and thoughts are worthy of global promotion. China is also a country worthy of global respect, contributing about 30 per cent to global economic growth in recent years, thus becoming the world's largest contributor to global economic expansion.

To pursue our national development, China and South Africa should not blindly copy the development models of other countries. Instead, we should rely on our own wisdom to cope with challenges in the course of development and find a new path with our own characteristics. This is the process when we, the intellectuals and think tanks scholars from our two respective countries, can contribute.

But we remain on a Long March. The history of the world has just begun. We, as members of think tanks from China and South Africa, should join hands and assist each other, and make contributions to the further development of our two great nations.

CHINA HAS THE ABILITY TO DEAL WITH AMERICAN PROVOCATION

AN EXCLUSIVE INTERVIEW WITH 'RUSSIA TODAY'

Donald Trump is an interesting person, he's very good at learning and now he's learning how to be a president of the United States. I don't think Trump should be analyzed on the basis of what he said during the election campaign. We need to give him time to learn. China has the confidence to deal with Trump and show him what is in the long-term core interests of the US. It is also in the interest of the US to cooperate with China, and the US with Russia.

On March 30, 2017, Dr. Wang Wen was invited to attend the Moscow Economic Forum and gave a keynote speech. He was interviewed by Russia Today *to discuss China's position on issues pertaining to Sino-US relations. This article is based on transcripts of the studio interview.*

Russia Today commentary: The United States is once again trying to show goodwill toward China. The Chinese president is preparing to pay a state visit to the US to meet his newly elected counterpart. However, at this point, tensions in the South China Sea are rising. With disrespectful words from both sides, where will China-US relations go? Last week, we learned about American views of the situation between China and the US. Today, March 30, 2017, we have the honor to have Dr. Wang Wen in the studio, a senior government adviser and executive director of Chongyang Institute for Financial Studies, Renmin University of China, and guest speaker of the current Moscow Economic Forum, to explore more about the Chinese side of the story.

Sophie Schawanazi: Welcome to our studio, Dr. Wang Wen. We understand that you are not only the executive director of the Chongyang Institute for Financial Studies, but also a senior adviser to the government. So, we would love to hear more from you on many topics today.

After a series of threats issued by the new US government to China, such as launching trade wars and driving China from artificial islands, the US seems to be trying to show goodwill to China. Does the Chinese side intend to start all over again by letting bygones be bygones?

Wang Wen: The handling of relations with the new US administration is a foreign policy priority for China. Next week, President Xi Jinping and President Trump will meet. This, I think, will start a new stage in the development of Sino-US relations.

Sophie Schawanazi: You mentioned the meeting to take place between the two heads of state at Mar-a-Lago resort in Palm Beach. What is China's expectation of this meeting?

Wang Wen: I think the US should learn from Russia. China and Russia have always respected each other. However, the US has not been friendly to China or Russia in the past. China hopes to use this meeting to tell the US that they should respect other powers such as China and Russia.

One of the great challenges facing Sino-US relations is how to avoid falling into the 'Thucydides trap' – when one power rises, another will wage war against it, or a war will break out between existing and emerging powers. China does not want to go to war with the US, and it hopes that the two countries can avoid this historical trap.

Sophie Schawanazi: I want to have some detail on how China can avoid a war. Although diplomatic rhetoric is always impeccable and exhilarating, it turns out that, when you go into detail, it doesn't work at all. Secretary of State Tillerson, for example, has claimed that China and the US follow the principle of 'no conflict, no confrontation', but there is no indication that the US Navy will stop patrolling in the South China Sea. Nor is there any sign that China will abandon its claims on the islands, meaning a confrontation between the two sides is inevitable.

Wang Wen: I think the issue of the South China Sea is very complex, and good negotiation and coordination channels exists between China and the US.

Sophie Schawanazi: What kind of channels are they?

Wang Wen: For example, when the US Secretary of State visits China, senior Chinese officials also visit the US to discuss these issues face to face, and then coordinate negotiations and deal with the crisis. I am in favor of this way of doing things. As a think tank scholar, I think China today has enough confidence to mediate with the US over the South China Sea issue.

Sophie Schawanazi: I interviewed a US Defense Department adviser the other day, and he told me that, in the US, some people want to have a showdown with China – that's what he said. Are there such hawks in China who want to engage in a full-scale, long-term confrontation with the US?

Wang Wen: On the issue of the South China Sea, the views of the US are very complex and there are many different voices...

Sophie Schawanazi: I'm not just talking about the South China Sea, but in the overall sense that there is now one group of people in the United States, including some possibly in government departments, who, for one reason or another, advocate confrontation with China. For example, it may be that China's rise will threaten the hegemonic position of the US in the coming years. Americans who hold such a position do exist. Are there any similar hawks in China?

Wang Wen: I don't think so. First of all, the US should not regard China as the next Iraq, Afghanistan or Libya. China is the second largest economy in the world. We are not afraid of empty remarks or statements by the US. China is strong enough to resist foreign aggression and smart enough to deal with these very polemical, sensational, threatening statements.

Sophie Schawanazi: But you didn't answer my question. Is there a similar argument for confrontation in China?

Wang Wen: Of course! The situation in China is very complicated. We have a population of 1.3bn and there are many nationalists. These nationalists are very tough on the US and dare to confront it. By contrast, China's government is sensible and wants to strike a balance between nationalism and liberalism and blaze its own trail of diplomacy. China wants peaceful, gradual and win-win relations with big powers.

Sophie Schawanazi: We'll talk about 'win-win' later, but I've heard more than once from China and the US that even a small accidental conflict could trigger an all-out military confrontation or even war. Is conflict a matter of time for the Chinese? Are you ready for this? After all, no one knows the future.

Wang Wen: Yes, China is ready to deal with any possible situation. On the one hand, China has many think tanks like ours that help the government to plan; on the other hand, our foreign policy-making is very wise. We are always capable of avoiding the worst. We should have confidence in China's foreign policy makers. For the past 30 years, China has not been at war with any country. China is the most peaceful country in the world.

Sophie Schawanazi: You just mentioned 'mutual respect'. These days, 'mutual respect' seems to be a popular term for the Chinese, which means that neither side will challenge the other's interests. But the US has its own traditional interests in the Asia-Pacific region, with Japan and other allies. Will China accept the status quo? Or is it going to be a challenge? Are you going to challenge the partnership between the US and Japan and South Korea?

Wang Wen: Yes, I understand that China's rise is game-changing. Its rise has changed the landscape of the Asia-Pacific region. Countries such as Japan and South Korea, as you mentioned, as well as others in Southeast Asia, are unable to adapt to the new situation. So I think China's diplomatic strategy is to handle relations with other countries and its neighbors very patiently, so that these countries will gradually adapt to the existence of China as a new power.

Sophie Schawanazi: The United States always says it will respect the 'one China' principle and will not try to change the status quo between the mainland and Taiwan, but the US acts in its own way. For example, the US is still selling arms to Taiwan. Is that acceptable to China?

Wang Wen: I think the 'one China' principle is the bottom line of China's foreign policy.

Sophie Schawanazi: How do you think that the US views the 'one China' principle?

Wang Wen: I think President Trump understands well enough the bottom line of China's foreign policy. He has never crossed that line since taking office. I take it as a sign of respect for the 'one China' principle. That's my understanding.

Sophie Schawanazi: But it is also true that the US is reportedly prepared to ship weapons to Taiwan on a large scale, ignoring China's warnings. Will China challenge this in some way? Are you going to make a serious response or are you just going to express your dissatisfaction verbally?

Wang Wen: Yes, China opposes US arms sales to Taiwan, but on the other hand, from a scholar's point of view, I firmly believe that the weapons sold by the US to Taiwan will eventually become China's spoils of war because Taiwan will return to the motherland in the future.

Sophie Schawanazi: But 'the future' is a very broad concept. Let's just talk about what is happening right now: Taiwan is growing militarily stronger thanks to the help of the US. Is it acceptable to you that it may take hundreds of years for China to achieve full reunification?

Wang Wen: I don't think so. Taiwan is an island. Even if Taiwan is militarily stronger than in the past, it is impossible to change the status quo of 'one China'. Mainland China's GDP and military power are dozens of times larger than those of Taiwan, so we have full confidence. As for the future, China has a long history of civilization, we have the wisdom and patience to observe and shape the future.

Sophie Schawanazi: The islands in the South China Sea, where China claims sovereignty, may soon become an airstrip for Chinese fighter jets. Do you think that China will be permanently garrisoning on those islands to defend its sovereignty?

Wang Wen: I think China has every right to protect its sovereignty on the islands in the South China Sea. That is our right as the owner, and no one can stop it. So why should the US interfere in the construction of the islands in the South China Sea? Many Chinese regard it as unreasonable and denounce American intervention. I think the most important thing for the world to understand is that the South China Sea is an issue between China and Southeast Asian countries.

Sophie Schawanazi: But it doesn't look so easy. I heard that Secretary of State Tillerson says that the US will stop China from entering its artificial islands – how do you respond to that? If what the US says is true, what are you going to do?

Wang Wen: The US always makes thoughtless comments on everything.

Sophie Schawanazi: You mean it is just empty talk?

Wang Wen: That's the way I we see it. The US makes indiscreet criticisms on everything in the world. It doesn't make any sense at all.

Sophie Schawanazi: So, you don't think there's any basis for action at all even when the United States says: "We're going to stop China from entering the artificial islands they're building."

Wang Wen: We reject and criticize this empty and mindless talk. We hope the US can balance its relations with claimant countries and remain silent on the issue of the South China Sea.

Sophie Schawanazi: What would China do if the US really took action to block China's entry into artificial islands?

Wang Wen: It depends on the specific actions. We have adequate measures to deal with the possible actions taken by the US. What we have to do now is to wait and observe its actions.

Sophie Schawanazi: We're seeing a trend, which is that the United States has been luring China's neighboring countries to becoming its allies, such as Vietnam, South Korea, Japan, and so on, but the Philippines is now breaking away from the United States and turning to China, even if there is a territorial dispute between China and the Philippines. How should China handle its relations with its neighbors?

Do you think neighboring countries will form a close alliance around China?

Wang Wen: I think it's very wise for the Philippines to turn to China. The Philippines has finally figured it out. In the past, the former Philippine president had too much faith in the US. But when the new president came to power, he realized that the US could only give the Philippines empty promises and that China could provide them with regular support. The Filipinos are smart. They know who the good people are and who the liars are. So I think it sets a good example for China's neighboring countries. I have full confidence in Vietnam, Malaysia and other countries, even South Korea and Japan.

Sophie Schawanazi: Looking at the situation, do you think the alliance between the US and the neighboring countries of China and the Pacific Rim is disintegrating?

Wang Wen: Judging from this new situation, the US military alliance in the Asia-Pacific region cannot play a role because we, in the Asia-Pacific region, should advocate sustainable development in the new century, especially when facing the new conditions. How to achieve sustainable development? The best way is not via a military alliance, but one that is capable of economic development, investment and infrastructure-building.

Sophie Schawanazi: We have talked a lot and heard a lot about Sino-American confrontation, but come to think of it, it's unimaginable for an average American to live without Chinese products. I mean, how can China and the US talk about confrontation in this context where economic ties are so close that neither side can afford to lose?

Wang Wen: With regard to Sino-US relations, we should not only focus on confrontation, but also see other aspects of the relationship between the two great powers. Each year, more than 6m people travel between the two countries. The volume of trade between us is close to US$600bn. This is the other side of the story. Now, China and the US are interdependent. I think the argument of confrontation has been created and sustained by the media. In reality, what the two countries advocate is peace, mutual assistance and a win-win situation. I travel to the US every year and feel that the average American person is the same as the average person in China. They believe that stability and peace are the common goals of the two countries.

Sophie Schawanazi: I want to talk about President Trump's withdrawal from the TPP. President Obama was very keen on the TPP and excluding China, and now President Xi Jinping has declared that he will defend free trade. Does this mean that China will take on the US's leadership role with regard to free trade?

Wang Wen: All countries should abide by WTO rules. We have established rules. Why does the US need to establish new rules? I think President Trump has done a good job. Most Chinese approve of the way Trump has conducted this business.

Sophie Schawanazi: I understand why China agrees with Trump's withdrawal from the TPP. It is clear that China, as a major country in the Asia-Pacific region, would feel uneasy about being excluded from such a major deal. But China has also launched a free trade agreement in the form of a regional comprehensive economic partnership agreement in the region. Does China welcome the United States in this regard?

Wang Wen: Join what?

Sophie Schawanazi: The Regional Comprehensive Economic Partnership Agreement (RCEP).

Wang Wen: Of course, we welcome the US very much. The core value of China's foreign policy today is win-win, open and inclusive. Therefore, we welcome all countries to join this China-sponsored agreement. For example, we have now the most important initiative – the Belt and Road initiative – which China welcomes all countries to join. I think Russia's active participation is commendable, while the US is still wavering.

Sophie Schawanazi: Another issue is that China has always been used to playing a leading role in the Asia-Pacific, but now we're seeing China building Silk Road infrastructure projects and investing heavily in Africa. Does this mean that China is breaking with its traditional diplomacy and seeking wider international influence?

Wang Wen: Of course, China is the second largest economy, and it will become the world's largest economy in the next decade. It will also become the world's largest consumer market in the next three to five years. So, of course China wants to provide more public goods to the international community. In the past, the world underestimated China's contribution to global governance. Three years ago, President Xi Jinping launched the Belt and Road initiative, which means that China, as an emerging power, hopes to contribute to the world under the premise of peace, win-win situation, and avoidance of conflict and war.

Sophie Schawanazi: Finally, I want to ask you a brief question about Trump. His attitude to China has been unclear, changing on a daily basis. Do you think this unpredictability is actually one of his strategies? If so, does it work for China?

Wang Wen: Trump is an interesting person, he's very good at learning and now he's learning how to be a president of the United States. I don't think Trump should be analyzed based on what he said during the campaign. We need to give him some time to learn. China has the confidence to deal with Trump and to show him what the long-term core interests of the US are.

Sophie Schawanazi: Thank you very much, Dr. Wang, for granting this interview. I wish you all the best.

CHINA TAKING THE LEAD IN THE CHINA, US AND RUSSIA TRIANGLE

In the complex and changing era of multi-polarization, 'positive balanced diplomacy' should be a wise choice for China. The process of strengthening coordination between the US and Russia to peacefully resolve the crises in North Korea and Syria characterizes the process of the rise of China as a great power with Chinese characteristics. Strengthening global policy coordination among China, the US and Russia, gradually reforming the current global system and mutually relieving their strategic pressures will directly determine the future world security situation.

On April 19, 2017, at the fourth 'Viewing the World Forum', sponsored by Guancha.cn, Dr. Wang Wen gave a keynote speech on 'The China-US-Russia triangle and the crises in Syria and North Korea'. This article is based on a translation of the transcript of that speech.

The crises in Syria and North Korea in the spring of 2017 have rekindled public attention in the long-ignored triangular relationship between China, the US and Russia. Some are concerned about an escalation of the Syrian and Korean crises, and that an outbreak of large-scale conflict and war in the region will drag the three powers into a state of confrontation. Or will Syria and North Korea fall into such serious domestic disorder, which will then spread to China, the US and Russia, that the three powers will be drawn into another Cold War?

From the point of view of the author, a new type of game and balance among the three countries is taking shape from the crises in Syria and North Korea, which has been highlighted again since President Trump took office. In the field of international security, there is a great possibility of a rare G3-induced inertia. Due to China's leadership, a delicate period of peace and balance in the international community will emerge, known as the G3 + Security Era.

The world has entered into a new era of power relations characterized by the game theory being played by China, the US and Russia.

The end of the second world war also brought to an end global domination by Europe and the US. The world gradually entered an era of the new great powers characterized by game theory being conducted by China, America and Russia, which has continued until now.

According to Henry Kissinger's theory of 'triangular strategy' put forward in the middle of the 20th century, relations between China, the US and the Soviet Union were an 'inverted triangle' before the end of the Cold War in 1990. In other words, Cold War competition between the US and the former Soviet Union not only dominated relations among the three countries and the global pattern of international relations in general, but also affected China's relations with foreign powers as well. From 1945 to early 1990, the 'inverted triangle' period was roughly divided into two phases. Before the 1980s, the Soviet-China 'sides' of the triangle were stronger, and China's 'one-sided' policy, namely its alliance with the former Soviet Union, made the United States appear weak. After the 1980s, following a diplomatic rapprochement between China and the United States, the US-China side of relations strengthened. The Soviet Union was on the defensive, and the situation didn't change until the disintegration of the former socialist republic. After the 1990s, the US became the world's sole superpower in the post-Cold War era, and relations among the three powers took the form of a 'positive triangle'. The United States was on top, above Russia and China, which were reduced to the two points below. That is to say, the United States became the head of a triangular relationship, dominating relations among nations in the post-Cold War world. Russia, as the successor of the former Soviet Union, once embraced the US at all levels, whereas China, which was sanctioned by the US in the early 1990s, also developed a 16-word policy towards the United States, including a policy of 'not engaging in confrontation'. In the early 21st century, after Vladimir Putin came to power, Russia gradually broke away from the policies of its most recent past associated with Boris Yeltsin and adopted a 'double-headed eagle' strategy. Russia began to 'look eastward' in order to strengthen relations with China. In 2014, Russia established a comprehensive strategic partnership of cooperation with China; then Russia began to support China's Belt and Road initiative in 2015. China-Russian relations have gradually become a model for relations between large countries.

In 2008, the international financial crisis forced the US to turn to China. China quickly overtook the US in terms of gross industrial product and total trade volume, and has gained momentum in catching up with the US in terms of GDP, military power and financial strength. At this point, the state of triangular remains the same, but the position of the three countries has gradually shifted. China began to move upward, and for the first time in history, it moved to the top of the triangle, and began to dominate the relationship between the US and Russia and the development of the global situation. "China has risen to the top of the strategic triangle among China, America and Russia," the French newspaper *Figaro* commented on April 11, 2017.

US and Russian dependence on China was unprecedented after 2017. It is precisely because China's strategic position has ascended to the top of the triangular relationship that the US and Russia are seeing unprecedented levels of dependence on China.

Russia now relies more on China than China does on Russia. Strategically, Russia's choice of mutual trust in China is not just a historic one, but also a deliberate rational choice made by Russian strategists. In his new book *The Crisis of the World Economic System and Sino-Russian Relations*, President Putin's adviser, and also a very accomplished Russian scholar, Sergey Glaziev, who visited Chongyang recently, argues that there are seven options for Russia's future: 1) to maintain the current status quo between China, the US and Russia; (2) to become a colony of the US; (3) to become a protectorate of China; (4) to be isolated and invaded; (5) to be isolated and mobilize the general public; (6) to form a Russia-China strategic partnership; (7) to form a China-US-Russia strategic partnership. Russia has the most comfortable, but unstable position. Glaziev says Option 6 is the most likely one to make a big difference, namely to assist Russia's development in a comprehensive way, in areas such as finance, investment and trade, but also in politics, security and strategy. A non-aligned quasi-ally relationship between China and Russia is taking shape.

An overlap of strategic interests between America and China is also the highest it has been in many years. For example, both China and the US hope to stop North Korea from developing nuclear weapons; both hope to reverse the strategic imbalance in trade; both hope to strengthen infrastructure cooperation, and both hope that the renminbi can show a trend of appreciation. It can be said that Trump's performance so far has been most positive for China. To quote President Xi's remarks:

> We have a thousand reasons to improve Sino-US relations, and there is no reason whatsoever to ruin our cooperative relations. Indeed, it is really hard to find a reason for mainstream American society turning against China. China and the US have become the largest trading partners. Our bilateral trade is not directly competitive, but highly complementary. As always, the Chinese proverb puts it best: when we combine, we both benefit, and when we fight, we both get hurt. All Trump's cards are on the table: trade talks, currency issues, Syrian missiles, the mother of all bombs in Afghanistan, and the carrier battle groups to deal with the denuclearization on the Korean peninsula. Early this past April, I conducted intensive interviews with top US think tank scholars in Washington for a re-mapping of the New Era in Sino-US relations. In my opinion, Trump's learning curve is still steep; he is still in his 'learning period' and 'being tested period'. Over the past two

months in office, Trump has been caught up in a spiral of major China-related issues. To many, Trump's cycle is characterized by 'taking a bold stance, then supplementing his understanding, restating his attitude, making another rash statement and replenishing his understanding'.

Regarding the China-US-Russia triangular relationship, Trump's adjustment takes three forms. In terms of Russia and China, Trump's 'test' has a somewhat self-imposed limit. On the issue of Syria and North Korea, his response towards China and Russia is extremely skeptical. Since he took office, for example, Trump has proved how different he is from traditional political figures: from being quick and aggressive to ruling with decisiveness and an iron fist, from reneging on his words to acting like a temperamental actor. But a closer look shows that the goals Mr. Trump wants to achieve are rarely abandoned easily, and that some reneging is nothing but a strategic retreat at a certain point in time. For example, repealing Obamacare and climate change policies, withdrawing from TPPs, repeatedly imposing injunctions and pushing for the construction of a 'Berlin Wall' along the US-Mexico border. But there are only two exceptions: one for China and the other for Russia.

Trump did not show any apparent malice against China. Despite previous setbacks, he eventually returned to the stance of successive US presidents on the Taiwan issue, which was considered a diplomatic victory for China. It has also accepted China's claims of a new type of power relationship initiated many years ago. It refused to participate in the protest against China's human rights record launched jointly by 11 Western ambassadors, which is extremely rare for the US.

Trump has also maintained a relatively moderate attitude towards Russia. Although improved relations between the US and Russia will weaken China's initiative against Russia, which is a legitimate concern of China, the Trump administration does feel the tension and pressure from Russia against the use of force against Syria. Trump has done even what Obama failed to accomplish; he almost single-handedly destroyed the possibility of improved Russia-US relations. Now, Trump is clearly switching course on US-Russia relations, because he does not want to see the bilateral relationship deteriorate, but to get back on the right track.

It can be concluded that, on the whole, the general tenor of China's foreign policy of 'seeking steady progress' and peacefully resolving international hot issues is guiding the process of resolving global problems. It also helps the major powers, including the US and Russia, avoid making misjudgments when seeking solutions to major international issues. This makes the solution of issues by force, which the US and Russia have often resorted to over the past decades, less viable. And by responding promptly to China's demands, the US and Russia have created the most favorable conditions for China's rise in a sustainable manner.

The G3 of China, the United States and Russia

In future, as a result of the coordination and guidance of China, the triangular relationship between China, the US and Russia has changed from a zero-sum game to one of competition and cooperation. The G3 are the key players to handle important and sensitive security issues, such as the issues of Syria and North Korea.

First, the triangular relationship between China, the US and Russia has changed from a linear zero-sum game to a complex competition game. The relationship among the three is not the same as the zero-sum game relations that existed between China, the US and the former Soviet Union in the Cold War era of East-West confrontation. Judging from the content of bilateral relations between China, the US and Russia, the situation has undergone fundamental change, surpassing the Cold War and transcending the zero-sum game, presenting itself in the form of the comprehensive great power coordination game. Second, the trilateral relationship takes on the form of a 'G3' state in issues concerning sensitive security, such as in Syria and North Korea. With the exception of the 59 missiles fired by the US, which makes no real difference, the three countries maintain 'chicken game' diplomacy, and coordination due to diplomatic boldness as a result of domestic factors. The status quo of the G3 game in future will determine the security of the world, and the greater the role China plays in guiding peace, the greater the prospect for global peace. War in North Korea in the foreseeable future is still a low-probability event; this is not only because of financial, military, security and other factors, but also because of the 'G3-plus' coordination model. The US and North Korea are rather like two provincial men from southern China trying to pick a fight. They yell at each other, but they don't exchange blows. Perhaps this is called rationality, Shanghai style. As a popular Shanghai saying goes: If you win the fight you end up in a court of law, but if you lose the fight, you go to hospital.

Third, although there are some conflicts of interests that cannot be reconciled in the short term between China, the US and Russia, the Sino-Russian strategic cooperative partnership, and the 'constructive', 'cooperative' and 'results-oriented' strategic partnership between China and the US, are taking on a new pattern of global power relations, thus rewriting the history of the rise and fall of great powers in international relations.

In future, the US may gradually abandon the Asia-Pacific rebalancing strategy and seek strategic deals with China. With the Eurasian Economic Union, an economic alliance initiated by President Putin that involves Belarus and Kazakhstan, Russia may hope to strengthen its integration with China's Belt and Road initiative. Under the great Belt and Road initiative, there is likely to be a better chance for cooperation between China, the US and Russia, in areas such as infrastructure construction, anti-terrorism and in curbing security incidents. This possibility, though not very high, is theoretically greater than a trilateral rupture between the three powers.

The recent US air strikes on Syria heightened tensions on the Korean peninsula and in the Middle East, and the upcoming presidential election in France has once again raised investor risk aversion. Meanwhile, international gold prices have risen frequently and gold funds have increased across the board. In future, gold funds will remain a good hedge against risks in the equity and bond markets and the long-term allocation of assets.

In the complex and changing era of multi-polarization, 'positive balanced diplomacy' would be a wise choice for China. Meanwhile, maintaining domestic and regional balance will make China's rise sustainable. The process of strengthening coordination with the US and Russia to peacefully resolve the crises in North Korea and Syria is a process through which a great power such as China will rise with Chinese characteristics.

Strengthening global policy coordination between China, the US and Russia, gradually reforming the current global system and mutually relieving their strategic pressures will directly determine future world security. With the strategic objectives of the three powers remaining unchanged, the forces of the three powers will remain in equilibrium.

IV

THERE'S NO NEED TO OVER-HYPE THE RISK OF THE BELT AND ROAD INITIATIVE

MACRO-RESEARCH ON BELT AND ROAD IS LARGELY CONCLUDED

Case studies, following cross-sectional macro-research, will shed more light on the role of the Belt and Road initiative. A few scholars have remarked that Belt and Road will entail a huge political risk. This remark should be analyzed from two perspectives. Risk prevention is important, but risk always promises the possibility of high profit. Businessmen are certainly smarter than scholars. They travel the world with their hard-earned money, exploring business opportunities in the Belt and Road countries and regions. They are the ones who know best where to go make a fortune, so their successful experience deserves careful academic study.

Sponsored by Chongyang Institute for Financial Studies, Renmin University of China, the Observer and Chunqiu Institute of Strategic Studies, the Belt and Road Initiative Nations' Data Map media briefing and seminar was held on April 8, 2015. More than a hundred delegates attended the event, including government officials, industry leaders, and friends from the press and media.

TODAY, MR. WEN YANG, OUR SENIOR RESEARCHER AND PRESTIGIOUS scholar at Chongyang Institute for Financial Studies, Renmin University of China, and a senior fellow at the Chunqiu Institute of Strategic Studies, will officially release his 'Belt and Road Macro Situation Distribution Map'. The map, which took nearly a year to complete, makes a very detailed quantitative analysis of the economies, energy, security and other areas of the Eurasian continent. This is a rather historic event for the study of China's Belt and Road initiative by think tank scholars. It may mean that macro environment study on Belt and Road has come to an end and is now officially entering the third stage that features the study of individual fields, along with area and case studies.

In 2013, during a to Kazakhstan and Indonesia, President Xi Jinping proposed the construction of 'One Belt', the Silk Road Economic Belt, and 'One Road', the 21st Century Maritime Silk Road. More than two and a half years have passed since then. Personally, I think that the first-stage study of the Belt and Road initiative has essentially been concluded and that we will soon enter the second stage. Why?

The first stage, which I call the macro study, focused on the general concept and significance of the Belt and Road initiative. In early 2015, Professor Wang Yiwei, a senior researcher at Chongyang Institute, published a monograph entitled *The Belt and Road Initiative: Opportunities and Challenges*. The book has been critically acclaimed in China and translated into English, Arabic and Polish. It is widely regarded as a representative work to come out during the first stage. Last year, William Jones, another senior foreign researcher at Chongyang, published a book *From the New Silk Road to the Eurasian Continental Bridge,* describing the meaning and concept of the Belt and Road initiative from an American perspective. Professor Wang Linggui of the Chinese Academy of Social Sciences has also compiled some books that include foreign experts' views on Belt and Road and the Asian Infrastructure Investment Bank. In addition, many television networks and websites have also broadcast shows and run articles that elaborate on the Belt and Road initiative. By early 2015, this phase of the study had essentially been completed. An official then in charge of the important decision-making work on the initiative suggested that studies should no longer focus on the importance of Belt and Road. I think this suggestion is quite reasonable because, over the past year or two, there have been too many articles on this subject. Of course, some people have criticized China for not understanding the challenge posed by the 'Belt and Road' project. I think this is mainly because of China's centuries-long closed-door policy during the Ming and Qing dynasties. From this point of view, I would refer to Belt and Road as China's fourth attempt to look at the world with eyes wide open.

The first attempt started with the Opium War back in 1840, as everyone knows. It was initiated by the first group of senior reform-minded officials with Western ideas, such as Lin Zexu and Wei Yuan. At the end of 19th century and into the early years of the 20th century, that is, after the First Sino-Japanese War of 1894 and the invasion of China by the Eight Allied Forces, it was officially declared that the Self-Strengthening Movement, the first attempt to 'see the world', had ended up in failure. At the same time, blind xenophobic riots such as the Boxer Rebellion took place.

The second one lasted from the Revolution of 1911 to the May 4th Movement in 1919, when China stated its intention to bring in two foreign gentlemen in the form of 'Mr. De' and 'Mr. Sai', representing democracy and science. As China came to realize the flaws in its own culture, it began to see the positive side of the West. It was determined not just to learn Western skills, but also to adopt its ways of problem solving. Unfortunately, 'Open your eyes and see the world' at that time was basically a copy of the West, and some even advocated the abolition of Chinese characters and the use of the Latin alphabet. As a result, China fell into the abyss of war and civil strife throughout the first half of 20th century. Until 1949, marked by Mao Zedong's essay *Farewell, Leighton Stuart*, China's socialist construction officially broke away from capitalism, and started all over again by rallying around the former Soviet Union. Yet, it is hard to evaluate the history of the subsequent 30 years in the history of contemporary China.

By the end of 1970s, China had entered the third round of reform and opening up. It was China's third attempt to see the world with eyes wide open. Once again, China looked to Europe, America and Japan, but its main goal was to introduce Western technology, management experience and capital. It should be said that this round of reform and opening up has been a great success. Of course, there have been many setbacks resulting from the fact that China focused too much on Western countries and not enough on its neighbors. Specifically, it failed to attach sufficient importance to Asia, Africa, Latin America, and other 'third world' countries as it did in the early years. The 2008 Financial Crisis, which originated in the US, has led China to realize that the Western system was seriously flawed and had major drawbacks. For the first time in human history, the GDP of emerging economies accounted for more than half of the world's total. At this crucial point in history, China begins seeking more cooperation with emerging economies than in the past, hence the BRICS summit mechanism, and enterprises shifting focus to countries in areas such as Central Asia, West Asia, Central and Eastern Europe, Africa and Latin America, and searching for potential new markets for cooperation in production capacity. The Belt and Road initiative came into being after the 18th National Congress of the CPC.

This long historical process also means that the Chinese world view has been upgraded and broadened, allowing China to realize for the first time that the world does not just comprise Western cultures, but emerging countries too, such as Iran, Turkey and states in Central Asia. Yet these countries were not in the Chinese collective consciousness. Even today when I sometimes ask my students in class, what is the capital city of Turkey? What are the five Central Asian countries? What are their capital cities? Most of them don't know. Therefore, this round of 'opening eyes to see the world' can be said to be the most profound since 1840 since it involved getting to know countries and regions that never interested us before. Over the past two years, many critics said that China's Belt and Road research is not profound enough. I disagree. In fact, China's think tanks have done a lot of research from scratch and on hot-spot issues. For example, by the end of 2015, in collaboration with a research team at Chongyang, I completed a project entitled 'A study of trade hub cities in Belt and Road countries'. Of course, Mr. Wen Yang is the most accomplished researcher in this field. Many experts, including those affiliated with the Chinese Academy of Social Sciences and the Development

Research Center of the State Council, have published a large number of works on the topic at the macro level.

In terms of macro research, there has been considerable scholarship and literature on topics such as how many countries are covered by Belt and Road research, what the situations are in the respective countries, including overall energy resources, economic development, financial stability, the security situation, and so on. It is like being approached by something ahead: is it an ape or human? Is it male or female? Is it fat or thin? Tall or short? So far, we have done thorough research on these issues.

Next, the key is how to conduct more detailed studies on some individual cases, countries and regions. Then, for example, if this object that is approaching from afar turns out to be human, we might want to examine whether he has heart disease, high blood pressure, or find out if he has a slipped disc and so on.

For example, in Mr. Wen Yang's macro distribution map, I think that at least one component can be added: 'ethnic composition'. If color is used to represent the different nationalities of a country, you will find that China is represented by a largely uniform, single color. Although there are 56 nationalities in China, the Han nationality makes up a large majority. But in Central Asia, multiple colors are used to represent the various Caucasian ethnic nationalities.

With the cross-sectional macro situation fully explained, additional vertical research on specific cases and projects will contribute more to the promotion of the Belt and Road initiative. For example, at Chongyang, we have generated some internal data based on which we analyze China's profit and loss situation of the 'Belt and Road' projects over the past decade or so. In the second half of the year, Chen Xiaochen, a full-time researcher at Chongyang, and I will publish a book tentatively entitled *The Belt and Road Strategic Map*. The book is based on field trips we took to more than 30 countries along 'Belt and Road'. The findings are based on our investigations of multiple projects in those countries. Some projects generate considerable profits, so the overall profit rate is very high.

But why do scholars in China fail to make sense of our findings? Some skeptical scholars remarked that the Belt and Road initiative would entail huge political risk. This remark should be analyzed from two perspectives. Risk prevention is important, but risk also promises the possibility of high profit. Businessmen are certainly smarter than scholars. They travel the world with their hard-earned money, exploring business opportunities in countries and regions along the Belt and Road. They are the ones who know most about where to make a fortune, so their successful experience deserves careful study by scholars.

If you are interested, we can all work together to promote the Belt and Road study and contribute our bit to China.

Again, thanks so much and congratulations to Prof. Wen Yang!

IT MIGHT BE USEFUL TO ESTABLISH 'BELT AND ROAD' STUDIES

―――

Based on the responses of various countries, the Belt and Road initiative has become the first topic emerging from China in recent years to lead global academic research and establish a worldwide agenda. This reflects China's growing soft power and international influence, as well as the world's growing enthusiasm and academic preference for Chinese solutions to global governance.

In early 2017, a number of seminars and forums were held in Beijing to prepare for the upcoming 'Belt and Road Summit Forum for International Cooperation'. Dr. Wang Wen has frequently called for the establishment of Belt and Road Studies at many forums. An abridged edition of this article was published in People's Daily *on January 23, 2017.*

At the World Economic Forum in Davos in May 2017, President Xi Jinping announced that China would host the Belt and Road Forum for International Cooperation in Beijing. The announcement sparked an upsurge in global interest and research into the Belt and Road initiative. Recently, a number of foreign embassy officials and think tank scholars have visited Chongyang or sent letters to make inquiries about the initiative. Belt and Road study may soon become a global school of 'learning'. Perhaps it is time to consider the idea of Belt and Road Studies.

In fact, the American think tank community has been studying Belt and Road in a comprehensive way since 2016. Almost all of the top American think tanks have started research projects relevant to the Belt and Road initiative, including projects pertaining to connectivity and geopolitics, infrastructure and development in Asia. Some study Chinese engineering projects along the Belt and Road by means of electronic remote sensing, data mapping, fund flow tracking and so on. Therefore, a new trend of academic research is emerging on the secrets behind China's 'going global' and its mounting influence on the world. Two books stand out: one by former US National Intelligence Council adviser Parag Khanna entitled *Connectography: Mapping the Future of Global Civilization*, the other by Oxford University Professor Peter Frankopan, entitled *The Silk Road*. The former boldly asserts that "infrastructure interconnection will be a country's greatest soft power in future", demonstrating that China's development experience has proven to be applicable to world economic development. This undoubtedly helps theorize the Belt and Road infrastructure study. The latter defined the Silk Road from the breadth of world history over the past 2,000 years and with solid and credible historical evidence showing that it has been referred to as the 'Road of faith', 'Road of Christ', 'Road to change', 'Road to harmony', 'Road to fur', etc. This is more like the Belt and Road historiography.

At the end of 2016, the Belt and Road initiative was first written into the United Nations General Assembly Resolution, reflecting the international community's general support and acceptance of the initiative. The Chinese academic community also analyzes the Belt and Road initiative in a systematic, theoretical and disciplined fashion, hence taking the lead in global research in this area. Therefore, China's academic community is blessed with a much stronger sense of responsibility and sense of mission to promote intellectual exchange between China and the world.

The greatest motivation for the development of social science comes from practical need. During the Spring and Autumn and Warring States periods, or at the time of the ancient Greek city states, there was no division of disciplines. In the 18th century, a division of labor system resulting from the Industrial Revolution promoted the division of social sciences and led to the classification of modern economics, political science, sociology and so on.

In the 20th century, the process of globalization was further accelerated, and the classification of disciplines became more detailed and focused on specific issues. For example, in 1919, after World War I, a special discipline known as 'international relations' was founded in Europe and the US; with the acceleration of monetary circulation and credit receipts and payments, 'international finance' gradually came into being. Some disciplines, such as 'Hongxue', literally Dream of the Red Chamber Studies, 'Dunhuang Xue', literally Dunhuang Studies, have become more and more popular. Some disciplines grow out of the needs of national development, the most typical of which are 'Marxist Colleges', which have been set up in almost all Chinese universities and colleges. In fact, Karl Marx once said that social sciences have always been pressed at the service of national development and ideology; Max Weber put it more bluntly, simply calling social science "the study of the state".

Judging from the responses of various countries, the Belt and Road initiative is the first Chinese discursive concept in many years to lead the world's academic research and set up a global agenda. This reflects China's growing soft power and international influence. It also reflects the world's enthusiasm and academic preference for China providing solutions to global governance.

It can be safely assumed that, if China does not set up Belt and Road Studies programs, our foreign counterparts will do so sooner or later. If that happens, Belt and Road Studies will experience the same awkward dilemma that relates to Dunhuang in China, namely, Dunhuang Studies being highly developed academically overseas; likewise, although *Dream of the Red Chamber* was written by the Chinese writer Cao Xueqin, academic study of the novel is much stronger abroad. This, I am sure you will agree with me, must not happen again.

In today's complex and complicated academic field, based on practical experience, Belt and Road Studies will aim to summarize the historical experience of China's engagement with the world, re-explain its interaction with the world, and re-evaluate future prospects for China's influence upon the world. This is bound to be a major theoretical and strategic project, and it will greatly facilitate the promotion of the Belt and Road initiative on a global scale.

Fortunately, several research institutions in China have set the Belt and Road initiative as a new direction in research for doctoral students, hence the emergence of Belt and Road Studies as an interdisciplinary and transnational study. If we take advantage of the Belt and Road Summit Forum for International Cooperation by setting aside Belt and Road funds for research, we can attract more scholars at home and abroad to contribute theoretically to the disciplinary construct of the Belt and Road initiative, and to guide the new round of global governance. Over time, Belt and Road Studies will improve the decision-making support system, public opinion guidance and enhance institutionalized discursive rights on the world stage, and it will continue to improve our entire person training methodology. Lastly, it will certainly become a new paradigm shift in global governance.

Based on Belt and Road Studies, the Chinese are bound to stand on new historical ground with a renewed sense of mission and responsibility, and to be more committed and more courageous, and to use China's own theoretical paradigm and discursive system to influence and change the world.

ON THE STRATEGIC ENDURANCE OF THE BELT AND ROAD INITIATIVE AFTER TRAVELLING TO FIFTY COUNTRIES

We should fully understand the brand value of the Belt and Road initiative, and then have the ability to plan, promote and manage the brand. We should also be able to explain the meaning and connotation of the initiative so that all countries march as one nation under the banner of global governance and international cooperation. It is high time for China to initiate this global undertaking, thereby allowing the nation to reach a consensus on the pursuit of the Belt and Road initiative, and then form a cohesive force. Only in this way, overseas, can we eliminate or reduce the possibility of politicizing our effort to build Belt and Road by the international community, hence producing a situation conducive to mutual consultation and joint construction.

In early 2017, a number of domestic and foreign organizations hosted seminars on the implementation of the Belt and Road initiative that had taken place over the previous three years. Dr. Wang Wen was invited to attend and present papers at many such events. This paper includes some of his major arguments and was published in the fifth issue of Frontline in 2017.

SINCE THE INCEPTION OF THE BELT AND ROAD INITIATIVE ABOUT THREE years ago, my colleagues and I have researched this book in nearly 50 countries, as well as in hundreds of counties and cities in China. At Chongyang, we have held hundreds of lectures, salons and seminars on the subject of Belt and Road. So far, eight volumes of selective essays have been published along with hundreds of newspaper and magazine articles. Our researchers have interviewed thousands of experts and professionals from all over the world. It is fair to say that we have kept ourselves informed with a great deal of up-to-date and first-hand information on the initiative.

The Belt and Road initiative has made more progress than expected over the past three years, but strategically it needs to be sustainable, and many basic concepts need clarification for long-term application. It is also necessary to constantly adjust the mutual expectation between China and foreign nations and avoid disorderly competition among all the provinces involved.

So far, the Belt and Road initiative has become China's most prominent brand name. Therefore, China should establish an overall coordination and comprehensive service mechanism as well as a research and evaluation mechanism so as to properly manage the brand. In addition, China should set up long-term transnational joint research groups, give full play to the role of key opinion leaders, renowned writers and new types of think tanks and tell a convincing story of the brand in order to promote the long-term development of the Belt and Road initiative.

Three prominent observations emerged after the research trip:

First, based on our research findings, we concluded that the Belt and Road initiative has indeed brought many practical benefits to participating countries along the Road, and the concept enjoys popular support in most of these countries. While some countries may be cautious, others are explicitly and extravagantly in favor.

Major powers, such as the United States, Japan and India, have a subtle attitude towards the Belt and Road initiative. The attitude of the US and Japan is subtle because they are constrained by their close bilateral relationship, while India is prone towards geopolitical considerations. Major countries covered by Belt and Road projects, including Russia and Turkey, have all bought into the initiative. A number of countries have also set up 'Silk Road ambassadors' who are held fully responsible for coordinating with China. However, it may take a while to implement existing projects and especially realize sustainable development.

Some countries' expectations for Belt and Road are too high. I have conducted some research in the Middle East where I found that the top concern is the actual benefits the initiative can bring to the region, without any mention of their own efforts. I also had the opportunity to participate in negotiations to finalize the text of a Belt and Road memorandum to be signed with a large country covered by Belt and Road projects. I observed that the other party was very keen to cram everything into Belt and Road-related projects. During the day-long negotiations, and having made numerous phone calls back to China to confirm the details with the competent departments of the projects, I discovered that many of the projects were nothing more than traps. Therefore, one has to be careful before signing contracts.

Second, through our research, we discovered that the Belt and Road initiative has generated enormous publicity around the world. Most political and economic elites in various countries have felt the influence of the initiative. But it will take a long time for Belt and Road to gain traction in the world and build true Chinese soft power, especially if some basic concepts are not fully agreed upon.

For example, some public media groups still go on about the concept of 'more than 60 countries involved in Belt and Road projects', which is why many foreigners ask about the identity of these countries. Are countries in West Africa and Latin America included? How important are the United States, Japan and South Korea to the Belt and Road initiative? In addition, the Chinese government prefers the Belt and Road initiative as the official translation, but for NGOs and in academic circles, they are more receptive to the term 'One Belt, One Road', while overseas the 'Silk Road Initiative' is preferred.

In 2016, I conducted two separate research projects on American views of the Belt and Road initiative. One was at the US State Department, where I briefed some middle-level officials on the Belt and Road initiative. The other was a jointly held US-China think tank dialogue on the initiative that was co-hosted by CSIS, a famous American think tank based in Washington DC. The most impressive and commonly asked question by the US side was: what is the difference between the Belt and Road initiative and China's 'going out' strategy that has been in place for quite a while? In India, I was questioned by my Indian counterpart, roughly to the effect: what are the geostrategic considerations for the Bangladesh-China-India-Myanmar corridor? The most frequently asked questions were: are Chinese companies making money in Belt and Road countries? How can risks be prevented? How does China intend to shift 'excess production capacity'? These questions require more convincing and comprehensive answers.

Our third finding was that there is a general consensus nowadays on the building of Belt and Road in various parts of China and this has all been written into provincial and municipal government work reports. But the projects implemented in various parts of the country are disorderly. Malignant competition is beginning to emerge, and some major projects lack sustainable profitability. Some local governments have gone to great lengths to subsidize their prestige projects.

For example, the China Railway Express (CR Express), which is an important part of the Belt and Road initiative and includes the Chengdu-Xinjiang-Europe, Chongqing-Xinjiang-Europe and Yiwu-Xinjiang-Europe lines, has made significant headway. But on the other hand, we need to consider whether there is a need for so many CR Express routes given the prospect of continued low shipping costs. And how do we ensure that the trains return from Europe with sufficiently high cargo volumes? To make matters worse, a survey has revealed a scandalous phenomenon known as 'snatching goods from all parts of the country'. In one city, the municipal government suggested that if goods are shipped from its city as the station of departure, it will pay for all the shipping charges of the freight delivered from any parts of the country. Then, another coastal city government promises to subsidize up to several thousands of renminbi per ton of goods. Foreign chambers of commerce jump at this opportunity, competing to ship their freight to where the city government provides the greatest subsidies. It is a shame that local governments have to support their prestige projects through public financing.

The above three findings show that, although the initial stage of the Belt and Road initiative has produced great results, bilateral and multilateral communication is still inadequate. Research and understanding also lack sufficient accuracy. Lastly, individual policies and projects are not well designed or developed. As a new, market-based initiative, especially a Chinese solution to the development issues of developing countries, the Belt and Road initiative must take into consideration sustainable and long-term development. Facts prove that our learning curve remains steep.

Managing the Belt and Road brand from the perspective of the future

All great powers in history have had a long-term grand strategy. In the case of the United States, for example, the Marshall Plan, which began in 1948 with the aim of advancing Europe's recovery after the second world war and strengthening the US-Europe relationship, was extended to the 1970s. The Marshall Plan was once considered a waste of money in America, but it played a vital role in the development of the US in the 20th century.

Yet, the Belt and Road's background and rules of operation are different from the Marshall Plan. In terms of coverage and global influence, Belt and Road is way ahead of the Marshall Plan. However, the US government's strategic endurance, determination and operational experience in promoting the Marshall Plan are worthy of China's reference.

For more than three years, the Belt and Road initiative has become a Chinese national brand. But if we aim to extend its life cycle for another 'two hundred years', we must constantly update our current brand management mechanism. As mentioned above, some Western media often interpret it from a geopolitical perspective, while several developing countries have expectations that are not quite in line with China's actual capacity. In addition, excessive marketing in certain parts of the country has also compromised the Belt and Road brand.

Therefore, we can only look to the future, draw upon the existing stock of experiences of other countries and take a long-term view before taking the next step in the Belt and Road initiative. With regard to the implementation and promotion of the initiative, China needs to establish a substantive overall and coordinated mechanism to comprehensively consider the various Belt and Road policy texts initiated by various ministries and commissions; to prevent policy conflicts among different departments, to restrain local governments from competing for resources and power, and to curb vicious competition among export-oriented enterprises.

For the sustainable development of Belt and Road's major projects, China needs to support the overall service mechanism for enterprises to 'go out', especially in investment banking, trust companies, law, consulting and research and development, etc. China should also establish a nationwide publicity services mechanism to glorify the image of the country, improve the livelihoods of local people, harmonize Sino-foreign relations and other aspects of our life. China should also institutionalize major security services to deal with emergencies, protect the Chinese diaspora, prevent the destruction of overseas property and other matters. For Belt and Road's overall brand management, not only does China need to have long-term thinking, but also a practical research and evaluation mechanism. In particular, on the basis of 'one country, one policy' and in the light of China's global strategy, we should conduct a comprehensive, objective and impartial third-party evaluation of the progress of Belt and Road projects, and summarize the risks and challenges encountered in the process and develop guidelines for future directions.

We should fully understand the brand value of the Belt and Road initiative. Specifically, we should plan, promote and manage its brand value; meanwhile, we should be able to explain the denotation and connotation of the initiative so that all countries march as one nation under the banner of global governance and international cooperation. It is high time for China to initiate this global undertaking. Only in this way, domestically, can the whole nation reach a consensus on the construction of Belt and Road, and then form a cohesive force; only in this way, overseas, can we eliminate or reduce the possibility of politicizing our effort to build the Belt and Road by the international community, hence producing a situation conducive to mutual consultation and joint construction.

Some recommendations

Over the past three years, the CPC Central Committee has been prudent and steady in promoting the implementation of the Belt and Road initiative. On various occasions, President Xi Jinping has made at least 200 references to it. At the beginning of 2015, the CPC Central Committee established a leading group on the One Belt and One Road Initiative. The National Development and Reform Commission (NDRC), the Ministry of Foreign Affairs and the Ministry of Commerce jointly issued an inter-agency directive, 'Advancing the Belt and Road Initiative: Vision and Action'. On this basis, we can look forward to the Belt and Road Summit Forum for International Cooperation to be held mid-May, 2017, which will feature a more authoritative, more comprehensive, more popular and more forward-looking basis for cooperation.

As a former prime minister of a Belt and Road country once said to me in private, the Belt and Road initiative represents a good offer, but you should not give the impression that you are foisting things upon countries covered by the project. Instead, Belt and Road's long-term development depends on imperceptible influence and long-term vision.

First, to launch the Belt and Road Joint Research Fund to attract global think tanks and academic institutions to contribute to research on the initiative, and to promote theorization and academic discipline. The establishment of Belt and Road Studies in the field of international intellectual and academic research will help summarize the historical experience of China's engagement with the world, re-explain the development in China's interaction with the world and re-evaluate the future prospects for China's influence upon the world. Belt and Road Studies will certainly improve the decision-making support system, shape public opinion and enhance institutionalized discursive power on the world stage, and continue to improve talents training methods and advance the process of China-led global governance.

Second, to give full play to the advantage of new media technology in the internet era and shape international public opinion on the Belt and Road initiative by means of multi-track communication. The target groups of the Belt and Road initiative should not be restricted to foreign governments but should also include business communities and the general public. Instead of relying solely on mainstream media, we should also look to the power of social media such as Twitter, Facebook and YouTube. In this respect, I joined some of China's social media VIPs on their trips to South America and Africa, and they had a very positive media impact. Against the background of a general decline in mainstream media influence and credibility, social media is an important way to shape international public opinion on the Belt and Road initiative, and also to win the hearts and minds of the people who live along the route.

Third, we should focus on several major literary projects by inviting a group of accomplished writers and think tank scholars to take part in the research. The idea is that more Belt and Road stories will feature in novels and international best-sellers. At present, millions of Chinese nationals are working hard in the Belt and Road regions to open up the frontiers for China's influence in the new era. In fact, the 21st century calls for more literati who can produce masterpieces on a par with Wei Wei, known for his classic war essay *Who is the Most Lovable Person*, and Ding Ling for her *The Sun Shines over the Sanggan River*. More important, China should also encourage some international best-selling writers such as Thomas L. Freedman whose *The World Is Flat* is selling well around the world, and Peter Frankopan, professor of global history at Oxford University who is known for his *The Silk Roads: A New History of the World*, to participate in the project because they tend to have an objective understanding of the Chinese, instead of pandering to China. They are the target of a new international united front and a new force to help publicize China in a positive light.

Fourth, we should strengthen the training of specialized talents for hire by Belt and Road-related projects, design a Belt and Road edition of central government schemes to recognize and recruit international scientific experts, known as the Thousand Talents Plan, or the Ten Thousand Talent Program, so that we can attract talents of all kinds from all over the world. Now, more than a million Chinese nationals are working in countries along the 'Belt and Road', many of whom are familiar with local culture, language and investment methods, and have deep connections with these places. They are truly rare talents who are in high demand. Meanwhile, China should also consider sending personnel with local expertise to all regions and countries where we can perhaps create positions and bodies such as commissioners, special envoys, industry associations and regional societies. We will continue to unswervingly push forward the implementation and coordination of the Belt and Road initiative.

In sum, we should uphold the idea of cooperation and opening up, and expound the market-oriented concept of joint development and risk-sharing in a practical and realistic way. By giving full play to the role of think tanks, countries covered by Belt and Road will eventually be incentivized by common interests to cooperate with China. In this way, with the joint efforts of many parties, I believe that 2017 will be another fruitful year for the Belt and Road initiative, and the road of Belt and Road will become broader and broader.

CHINA-US COOPERATION ON THE BELT AND ROAD CAN BEGIN WITH REPAIRING NEW YORK'S ROADS

China's initiatives and actions are more peaceful, inclusive and constructive than any rising power in history. It exports no disasters, no wars, no refugees, no conflicts, but instead exports goods, infrastructure, trade, investment and hundreds of millions of tourists. The 'peaceful' rise of such a big country is not made possible by starting a revolution, but by maintaining the status quo. In the US, most scholars have to admit that China is at least the most important power to have maintained the international order since World War II.

In June 2017, with the support of the Chinese Public Diplomacy Association and the Chinese Consulate General in New York, four rounds of discussions and seminars on the Belt and Road initiative were held at the United States Council on Foreign Relations, the offices of Bloomberg News, the National Committee on US-China Relations and the University of Pennsylvania. As one of the four Chinese experts invited to these events, Dr. Wang Wen, executive director of the Chongyang Institute for Financial Studies, Renmin University of China, made several keynote speeches and highlighted the progress of Belt and Road during the events. The text of this paper is based on a translation of the transcript of one of the speeches.

On June 22, 2017, US President Donald Trump made clear for the first time that the United States was willing to participate in the Belt and Road initiative when he met with Chinese State Councilor Yang Jiechi in Washington DC. Yang was attending the first round of the China-US Diplomatic Security Dialogue. This was a major signal in the development of Sino-US relations, inseparable from the joint efforts made by those of vision from the two countries, as well as from the previous rounds of communication between think tanks in China and the United States.

The Chongyang Institute for Financial Studies, Renmin University of China is one of the Chinese think tanks that conducts the most exchange programs with their counterparts in the United States. The following is the full text of Dr. Wang Wen's speech made at one of the events.

For many, New York is the business capital of the world, because over the past 100 years, it has always been able to identify and profit from global investment, trade and financial opportunities, thus creating the splendor, or even the miracle, of an international metropolis. For China, over the past 40 years, venture capitalists in New York, especially those on Wall Street, have rightly found opportunities thanks to China's reform and opening up. By helping Chinese companies with financing, IPOs, M&A, reinvestment and other areas, they have made a considerable profit, while at the same time contributing to China's economic development, creating a win-win situation.

So, what about the China opportunity in the next 40 years? The opportunity lies in the Belt and Road initiative! Only when New York discovers the opportunity of Belt and Road, as it did with reform and opening up, can it carry on its 20th century glory into the 21st century. However, it is a shame that, in both New York and across the United States in general, public opinion, in my view, overestimates China's strategic ambitions with the Belt and Road initiative. They speculate that China is trying to create a new global order to replace the international liberal order spearheaded by the United States since World War II. I think this view is groundless, and wrong. On the other hand, US public opinion has also underestimated the potential for cooperation between China and the United States on the Belt and Road initiative. China can provide money, labor, infrastructure technology, and so on, for Belt and

Road projects, and so can the United States. The Belt and Road initiative provides regional security, international management experience and soft power. China and the US can help each other build the Belt and Road, so the US has good reason to become a stakeholder in the project and cooperate with China for a win-win outcome, and at the same time benefit other countries, thus creating a situation conducive to multilateralism characterized by a win-win for multiple parties.

Of course, it is normal for the United States to have different voices. It is not hard to imagine that some American people are skeptical about Belt and Road. Perhaps they do not know the initiative very well, or are poorly informed about how other countries evaluate Belt and Road's real progress. Over the past three or four years, my colleagues and I have visited about 50 countries to research the Belt and Road initiative. We have developed a strong sense of the world's expectation for China's contribution, and have come to make sense of the world's willingness to cooperate with China. Now, more than 120 countries and international organizations have expressed their support for the initiative and more than 40 countries have signed memorandums to co-build the Belt and Road with China.

Heads of state from 29 countries and representatives from more than 130 countries attended the Belt and Road Summit Forum for International Cooperation which was concluded this past May. This was the best attended international conference since World War II, on a par with the United Nations General Assembly conference in terms of the number of participants. All this demonstrates the international community's enthusiasm to participate in the Belt and Road initiative.

The Trump administration also sent senior delegates to the forum. In spite of the absence of high-level officials, Trump is more proactive toward the Belt and Road initiative than Obama. Two weeks ago, the California Governor Jerry Brown visited China and was received by President Xi Jinping. Brown expressed his readiness to take an active part in pursuing the Belt and Road initiative.

Just now, some friends shared their confusion about the Belt and Road's geopolitical intentions and their concerns about issues such as human rights, environmental protection, business transparency and legal standards. I am fully aware of the fact that there are some disappointments about the Belt and Road's implementation. However, more than three million Chinese companies are currently operating overseas, and the vast majority of them are private businesses. It is impossible for such a large group not to be accused and criticized for imperfections. But if we look for small-scale flaws, we may totally miss the beauty of the world.

In my opinion, the United States, especially the investors, researchers and social elites in New York, can identify the opportunity presented by the Belt and Road initiative on condition that it should fully accept the rise of a China with a global strategic initiative, vision and policy. Yet, China's rise is real. As the second largest global economy, likely to become the world's largest in the foreseeable future, China will inevitably come out with global actions and initiatives.

But China's initiatives and actions are more peaceful, inclusive and constructive than those rising powers in history. China exports no disasters, no wars, no refugees, no conflicts. What we do export are goods, infrastructure, trade, investment, and hundreds of millions of outbound tourists. The 'peaceful' rise of such a great power is not meant to break radically away from the status quo, but to maintain the status quo. In the United States, most scholars may have to admit that China has been at least one of the most important powers to maintain the international order since World War II. Just now, some American friends mentioned China's vagueness about the Belt and Road initiative and asked whether Latin America would be included. Indeed, China's understanding of the Belt and Road initiative has been constantly changing over the past four years, in response to the progress made during the process. For example, at the beginning, the Belt and Road initiative mainly focused on the Eurasian continent. In its foreign statements, the Chinese government often stated that there were '65 Belt and Road countries'. Later, as the world became more receptive to the initiative, including countries such as Australia, New Zealand and those in Latin America and Africa, it has quickly evolved into a global initiative.

This is precisely the Chinese learning process through global interaction, reflecting the spirit of learning by doing. Not long ago, I wrote a long article about China's 'worldview', which elaborates on the fact that China would no longer look to the West only, but instead would start to look around the world. Historically, from the Qing dynasty, when it closed its door to the outside world, China considered itself the Central Kingdom; when the People's Republic of China, aka the New China, was founded in 1949, China's foreign policy initially focused on its solidarity with the former Soviet Union and the former socialist bloc nations; yet, during the early days of reform and opening up to the outside world since the late 1970s, China focused on cooperation with the West. Finally, the proposal and promotion of the Belt and Road initiative represents the evolution of the Chinese world outlook. If you don't look at China from a historical perspective, perhaps you can't understand it.

The success of China's reform and opening up can be said to embody the spirit of 'learning by doing', or 'crossing the river by feeling the stones'. Based on this, a friend from the United States posed the question: what would happen to the Belt and Road initiative five years from now? I think this is extremely hard to predict. Consider this: just 40 years ago, no one could have imagined that reform and opening up would make such a big difference in China. When the Belt and Road initiative was first proposed, I am afraid even President Xi himself could not contemplate the progress that has been made so far. He has said in public on multiple occasions that "progress has exceeded our expectations" four years since its inception. From this point of view, perhaps in five years' time, the Belt and Road initiative will also make more surprising progress than we now anticipate. However, as Chinese, we are good at making five-year plans. According to the Chinese government's public commitments and plans, some of the data are very noteworthy. Since the beginning of this year, China's government has stated many times that China will import US$8tn-worth of goods and invest US$750bn in the world, and a cumulative total of 130m Chinese are expected to travel abroad in the next five years. My friends in New York, please imagine, how many business and investment opportunities that presents, which in turn, would allow you to make profit. Some of you also talk about 'risk' and are curious to know how China manages it. To be honest, this should not be a question raised by New Yorkers working on Wall Street. Because, for Wall Street, doesn't risk mean profit? The greater the risk, the bigger the profit. How can a New York venture capitalist worry so much about risk? This may be a joke, but the logic is serious.

On the other hand, China's current financial resilience and investment capabilities are, in many cases, larger and stronger than those of the United States. Chinese companies seldom expect to make a profit in a year or two, but instead look at longer-term returns on investment. Infrastructure construction projects, in particular, tend to take a decade or two to make a profit.

But the fact that more infrastructure projects would lead to a rise in land prices and may affect people's livelihoods are worthy of attention. This 'consolidated profit' is a matter that merits our concern.

In this respect, China usually uses the 'industrial park' model to support long-term operations abroad. As the world's largest development bank, China Development Bank's non-performing loan ratio has remained below 1 per cent for a decade, which in itself is a sign of the success of the business model. Now, there is a new term in the Chinese lexicon – 'patient capital'. That's basically what the phrase tries to explain.

Back here in New York, I have shuttled between a number of organizations today. Unfortunately, the roads were very bumpy, so bumpy that I even developed a stomach ache. I am also aware of the fact that this problem has existed for years. Why not hire Chinese companies to repair the New York roads? I have full confidence that Chinese construction companies could do an excellent job. Perhaps, China-US cooperation in the Belt and Road initiative can begin with repairing this city's roads.

AN ANALYSIS OF THE BELT AND ROAD INITIATIVE THROUGH TEN PERSONAL STORIES

China's pursuit of cooperation through the Belt and Road initiative is not a pro bono undertaking. It aims at a win-win for all, which is to win and let win. The world is facing a long-term downturn in economic growth, sluggish trade growth and backward infrastructure in various countries. China's successful development experience since reform and opening up will contribute to the future of the world. More and more countries are actively seeking cooperation with China. Thus, China needs to be more proactive. This should be an important practice in the future Belt and Road implementation process.

This article was published in the overseas edition of People's Daily *on May 10, 2017.*

WHAT THE BELT AND ROAD INITIATIVE HAS ACCOMPLISHED OVER THE PAST three years has become a focus of public debate at home and abroad. A large number of media reports and academic studies tend to generalize with grand narratives and different data, but often ignore the multi-faceted stories behind the initiative. My colleagues and I at Chongyang have been traveling extensively in more than 40 countries to publicize, discuss and attend conferences on Belt and Road, and we have published numerous papers and articles to theorize the initiative. This time around, I want to offer an insightful analysis of the complexity and challenge of the Belt and Road initiative with 10 short, yet personal stories.

Don't take on all things

Story 1: As one of three Chinese negotiators working on drawing up the text of a bilateral memorandum of joint construction, I was nervously sitting at the negotiating table with representatives from a major country in the region. Issues of principle in the text were fairly easy to resolve, but negotiations on the specific details of major projects were in gridlock. The negotiators on the other side of the table were eager to use the Belt and Road initiative as a major opportunity to expand their own economy, cramming many major domestic projects into the memorandum; Chinese negotiators had to phone Beijing to seek help from competent agencies on each of the newly added projects.

Such talks are happy reminders that the Belt and Road initiative is extremely popular among the majority of countries in the world, but they also show that we need to guard against excessive expectations from some countries and the 'take-on-all-things' mentality in cooperative projects. In the first three years, China managed to sign memorandums of cooperation with more than 40 countries in order to promote the initiative on a faster track. Thus far, the Belt and Road initiative has won the public support of more than 100 countries and international organizations. Therefore, China should press ahead with the next round of opening up and maintain the momentum in its current effort to enhance and strengthen the global influence of Belt and Road.

Next, don't bite off more than you can chew. China needs to guard against taking on more than it can handle, although we still want to undertake big projects, sign big agreements, seek the support of big countries. More important, though, we should also take on small projects, pay attention to small details and eradicate small mistakes. After all, we have made major headways in the current stages of the Belt and Road initiative. It is imperative to take care of the details of projects across the world.

Guard against conceit and impetuosity

Story 2: In Kenya, the author surveyed the first railway built in the country's 100-year history, the one that departs from the largest port city of Mombasa to Nairobi, the capital city. The railway was built entirely by Chinese companies. Both locals and the local officials we interviewed were grateful to China and have full confidence in the Chinese system to operate the railway in future, thus giving the Chinese companies the right to operate for many years to come. They also hope that China can help to achieve sustainable and independent development of Kenya's economy. But surprisingly, companies from a certain country have invested in roads and related infrastructure along the railway line, in an attempt to compete against the Mombasa-Nairobi line. This project is a wake-up call in that, after making breakthroughs in many major projects covered by the Belt and Road initiative, we should continue to guard against complacency and impetuosity. Chinese companies both make and share the cake with Western enterprises in the global market with high quality goods through win-win cooperation and so on, which demonstrates China's ever-expanding soft power, but it also causes Western enterprises' vigilance, competition and even a backlash from the market.

Doing business in a new country by securing some big projects is like 'setting up startup businesses around the world'. In Chinese there is a saying: "It is easier to start up a business in China than to keep it prosperous." The road to China's rise is bound to be uneven, the path of Chinese enterprises to succeed in the world will not be easy and the implementation process of the Belt and Road initiative is bound to be bumpy.

Companies that benefit from Belt and Road are seeking a new birth

Story 3: Yiwu in Zhejiang province is an important trade hub along the Belt and Road. For many years in a row, the city's foreign trade has been growing at a double-digit rate. In 2015, the total volume of its imports and exports increased by 41.5 per cent, which is undoubtedly a great accomplishment in the context of a global trade average growth rate of about 3 per cent. Local officials and merchants told me that Yiwu's wholesale commodities were both high quality and cheap, which is quite different from European and American luxury brands. Therefore, Belt and Road is well suited to the consumer needs of developing countries. Two years ago, the 'Yiwu-Xinjiang-Europe' express train came into operation, and now hundreds of freight trains are running back and forth from Yiwu to Europe. In Yiwu Commodity City, a special 'hall for imported goods' has started business. That means that Yiwu residents can buy products from dozens of countries without leaving their home city. Yiwu has truly benefitted from the Belt and Road initiative.

This typical case reflects the pragmatism of the Belt and Road initiative. Many local enterprises, especially tens of millions of small and medium-sized business owners, treasure the idea of 'seeking to improve their business'. They hope that, in future, they can use the Belt and Road initiative to judge the hour and size up the situation to seek a new birth, or to put it in other way, a Phoenix Nirvana. At this point, it is a major responsibility of governments at all levels to face the following issues: how to comprehensively deepen reform, provide preferential policies and create conditions to help many small and medium-sized enterprises with smooth transformation and upgrading.

Not to give away profit, but a win-win for all

Story 4: In 2015, I was visiting an important think tank in Poland on a research tour. As soon as I was seated, my Polish counterpart joked: "You are the fourth Chinese delegation we have received this week, and I understand you are also here to talk about the Belt and Road initiative. We'd like to ask one question: what are the real benefits that China can bring to Poland?" In the conversations that followed, the Polish side repeatedly asked about the practical benefits China can bring.

This question remains fresh in the memory. Like a fishbone stuck in one's throat, I find it necessary to give vent to this pent-up feeling of mine. At present, most Belt and Road research and scholarship and business policy overtly emphasize bringing benefits to the other sides for fear that the other sides will not cooperate with us. This desire represents the sincerity and goodwill of China as it tries to involve the world in its development process. However, it must be noted that similar goodwill and sincerity sometimes breeds prejudice that may lead the world to misinterpret China's willingness to cooperate on its own initiative, which counterproductively suggests that China is asking for their help. As a matter of fact, China's 'going global' is all about satisfying mutual needs, not granting one-sided favors. But more often than not, China is 'Party A' in the cooperation contract. The Belt and Road initiative's pursuit of cooperation does not mean China has to give up profit. Instead, it aims at a win-win for all, which is to win and let win. The world is facing a long-term downturn in economic growth, sluggish trade growth and backward infrastructure in various countries. China's successful development experience since reform and opening up will contribute to the future development of the world. More and more countries are actively seeking cooperation with China. Therefore, China needs to be more proactive. This should be an important rule guiding the future Belt and Road implementation process.

Improving the rules of 'going global'

Story 5: While researching this book in a certain country in Latin America, I asked a senior executive from a state-owned Chinese company who his biggest competitor was. To my surprise, he did not identify any companies from the United States, Japan or Europe; instead, he pointed me to certain Chinese companies in the same sector. He complained about the embarrassing fact that Chinese companies tend to compete on price in the bidding process for projects.

"Chinese companies are not afraid to compete with any competitors from developed countries, but they are afraid to compete with domestic companies," he said. This left me dumbfounded. He hinted that domestic companies would sometimes get involved in vicious competition against each other and fail to abide by the rules of the game. This kind of competition is, of course, not only the result of marketization when Chinese enterprises are 'going global', but also reflects the blind pursuit of growth of some companies spreading their wings against the backdrop of the Belt and Road initiative as well as 'pursuing market share' as their only strategic goal. Therefore, it has become a top priority for companies participating in Belt and Road to continue to improve their management system, and strengthen sector management and rulemaking in the process of their expansion overseas. Ideally, this can help upgrade the branding of Chinese enterprises and turn them into what we call in Chinese, century-old brands.

External communication needs supply-side reform

Story 6: In Salzburg, Austria, I was giving a talk on the Belt and Road initiative to hundreds of entrepreneurs, heads of local chambers of commerce and government officials from Central Europe. After the talk, the vice governor of Salzburg said to me, with considerable gratitude, that he had not expected the delegates to listen to my two-hour talk so attentively. They were very interested to hear about so many true stories and the actual implementation of the Belt and Road initiative. The questions raised by some entrepreneurs were rudimentary: for example, how was the Belt and Road Initiative initially conceived? What is involved in the initiative and how long will the process last? This poor level of understanding reflects a general lack of theorizing and information-sharing with the rest of the world on China's part.

Many scholars who have been on overseas lecture tours have quite similar experiences, which I believe has increased the pressure on China's outreach and communication efforts. I have been lecturing on Belt and Road in dozens of countries, and what made me feel confused was not the hot heads in the audience who threw tough questions at me, but rather the limited knowledge of the Belt and Road initiative that exists despite a great thirst for such information. Over the years, millions of news reports in China have covered the Belt and Road initiative, but the effectiveness and breadth of communication through foreign languages is still insufficient. Therefore, it is a matter of urgency to know how to use new media and new technology to spread Chinese information far and wide; specifically, how to employ media such as movies and literature to tell our stories of Belt and Road so that we can win the hearts and minds of the people across the world. There is a long way to go when it comes to deepening supply-side reforms in the field of external communication such as narrative strategy, communication mechanism, operation and personnel.

Improving our view of geopolitics from the psychological perspective

Story 7: In Astana, Kazakhstan's capital, several local scholars lament the fact that, while the Belt and Road initiative has brought China and Kazakhstan closer, many Kazakhs still feel closer to Europe psychologically. In fact, it only takes an hour to fly to Urumqi from Almaty, Kazakhstan's largest city. Whereas in China, the situation is equally dispiriting. I once asked a class of graduate students to name the capital cities of the five Central Asian countries. The result was astonishing: not a single student could answer straight away.

This lack of knowledge is a reflection of China's social psychology. For most Chinese, abroad usually refers to developed countries such as the US, Japan, South Korea and those in Western Europe, while the presence of most neighboring countries is ignored, especially those in Central Asia. To put it another way, Belt and Road countries remains a huge 'blind spot' in the psychology of the Chinese public, which is an important manifestation of the imbalance of China's global outlook. Nowadays, more and more countries adopt a visa-free policy to China, or operate landing visas, which provides China with an important opportunity to adjust its national psychology. Ordinary people should be encouraged to interact more with their counterparts in neighboring countries, travel more to Belt and Road countries for sightseeing, and broaden the geographical vision previously constrained by Chinese parochialism. This is also a major focus of our effort in administering the Belt and Road initiative. If we can do this better, we can win the hearts and minds of the people living in countries covered by the Belt and Road project.

Direct currency arrangements starting to pay off

Story 8: Over the years, I have been visiting countries such as Thailand and Malaysia where I find consumers can directly spend renminbi at scenic spots and in some shopping malls; some businesses even price in renminbi. During the spring festival, more flights operate between Bangkok and Beijing than between Beijing and Shanghai, known as the busiest route in China. The Belt and Road initiative, which leads to more people-to-people exchanges, has a great advantage in Southeast Asia, making funding even more available. Not only in famous scenic spots in Southeast Asian countries, but also at similar sites in Egypt, Ethiopia and other African countries, I found that almost all the locals greet the Chinese tourists with "hello" and "thank you".

Commercial interaction is just the beginning. China has concluded direct currency deals with 23 countries, but only eight are from countries along the route of the Belt and Road initiative. Like blood circulating in the human body, financial cooperation aimed at accommodation of fund helps ensure the economic operational stability of the Belt and Road initiative. It is an indispensable part of 'the five aspects of connectivity', which is the core element of the Belt and Road initiative.

However, compared with policy communication, facilities connectivity, trade facilitation and popular support, it seems that direct currency deals, which is one of the 'five aspects of connectivity' in the Belt and Road initiative, has just begun to work. Promoting renminbi internationalization, facilitating trade and investment, and making financial cooperation a new engine of the Belt and Road initiative, should be a logical outcome.

Resolving disputes among the Great Powers

Story 9: In the summer of 2016, a grand global think tank conference was held in Mumbai, India, where global governance was the central topic of discussion. When it came to infrastructure construction, some Indian scholars expressed great admiration for and praise of China's contribution.

"I really want to go to China," a taxi driver told me. "China is richer than India, but India will get better and better in future."

"We have dreams, too, like the characters in the movie *Slumdog Millionaire*," said a Hindu slum-dweller. But when it comes to the Belt and Road initiative, they seem a bit restrained. Most Indian think tanks have their own and different ideas about the China-Pakistan Economic Corridor, the Bengal-India-Myanmar Economic Corridor, which complicates the implementation process of the South Asian segment of the Belt and Road project.

Likewise, some scholars in regional powers such as Germany in Europe and Turkey in East Asia remain particularly concerned about the consequences of the initiative. On the one hand, they approve of cooperation with China, riding with China's economic growth, learning from China's development experience and benefiting from its experience. At the same time, they are also anxious about China's growing geopolitical influence for fear that China will overexert its influence in the region. In fact, the Belt and Road initiative is not a zero-sum game; on the contrary, it is the embodiment of win-win value, and the principle of mutual consultation, joint-venture and sharing. Therefore, it has become a matter of urgency in terms of winning the hearts and minds of people around the globe.

Promoting a new cause on a global scale

Story 10: On April 18, 2016, my organization and the famous American think tank CSIS co-hosted the China-American Think Tank Dialogue on the Belt and Road Initiative.

This was said to be the first China-US dialogue on the Belt and Road initiative held in Washington DC, with hundreds of officials, scholars and officials attending the launch of the Dialogue's press release. One official said in response to the press release that a dialogue of this nature was now possible because the United States had begun to think seriously about the Belt and Road Initiative.

More than a year ago, I was invited by the US State Department to give two separate talks on the Belt and Road initiative. Several mid-level officials questioned the logic of the initiative even though they did not completely reject it. In fact, they were really eager to understand the true motivation behind Belt and Road.

This feedback has been corroborated in recent exchanges between China and the United States. Over the past few years, dozens of highly publicized US think tank reports have shown that different US administrations, especially the Trump administration, have changed their mind regarding the Belt and Road initiative. In 2017, at the 'Xi-Trump meeting' in early April, President Xi Jinping extended his welcome to the United States to join up with the Belt and Road initiative. This was China extending an olive branch to the United States, and a most positive response was received from his US counterpart. It can be predicted that the chances of major cooperation between China and the United States on the Belt and Road initiative are increasing, which will further advance new global progress of the Belt and Road initiative.

V

DON'T BE TOO PESSIMISTIC ABOUT CHINA'S ECONOMY

CHINA IS ENTERING ITS GREATEST FINANCIAL ERA

'Made in China 2025' helps lay the foundation of a great financial era in China, while the Belt and Road initiative helps create the external environment of a great financial era outside China. But I personally feel that I should use the word 'greatest', because never before in the history of China's 5,000-year-long civilization has the country's influence ever been felt in every single corner of the world, plus the fact that the influence is also increasing dramatically.

The annual China Finance and Economics Summit was held in Beijing on July 22, 2015. Dr. Wang Wen attended the summit and delivered a keynote speech.

2015 WAS DESTINED TO BE A SIGNIFICANT YEAR IN CHINESE HISTORY, AND even in world history. The meaning of this great significance is unknown to the present generation and will not necessarily be known to future generations. But there will always be wise, sophisticated historians who will discover the great significance of 2015.

In 1587, the fifteenth year of Emperor Wanli's reign during the Ming dynasty, Huang Renyu came to the conclusion that China was poor at using mathematics as a social management tool, and he regarded this as a national weakness. This weakness, along with some trivial events, dragged China into hundreds of years of recession. By the same token, more and more international relations scholars came to understand the true meaning of 1896. In 1894, the US's gross industrial product surpassed that of Britain, the same year that Henry Ford, an American, built his first four-wheeled car. At the same time, many countries began to build their own automobile industry. Subsequently, diesel locomotives, ocean-going ships and aircraft, all powered by the internal combustion engine, continued to emerge. The US achieved what it wanted to accomplish: one hundred years of global dominance.

So what happened in 2015?

In 2015, China announced its strategy known as 'Made in China 2025'. This is the first 10-year action plan to guide China in implementing a strategy of turning the country into a manufacturing power, and China's version of 'Industry 4.0', a plan aimed to establish China as a manufacturing power and a leader in global manufacturing. That is to say, over the past half century, China has truly transitioned from mechanization to automation, passing over electronization, and is advancing towards fourth-generation industrial systems featuring artificial intelligence. Manufacturing is a vital organ of a country, like the heart and kidneys in a human body. Don't underestimate it, because many medium-level powers have yet to build a complete manufacturing industry.

In 2015, China's Belt and Road initiative entered the implementation period. Early that same year, the leading group of the Belt and Road initiative was set up officially. On March 28, *The Belt and Road Vision and Action Plan* was officially published. In April, President Xi Jinping signed a US$46bn investment cooperation contract with Pakistan. Now, almost every provincial and city government, every ministry and department has developed its own version of Belt and Road. Some people may be concerned that the initiative entails considerable risk, or perhaps be no more than a vanity project. Such concerns may be well-intentioned, but they lack strategic consideration. It belittles the ambitions of our country's leadership.

In 1947, the US gave more than US$13bn in economic assistance to help rebuild Western European economies and financial systems after the end of World War II. This was equivalent to 5 per cent of its GDP. In the early 1980s, the Japanese government executed the 'capital recycling program', which involved spending US$60bn in aid, also accounting for 5 per cent of its GDP. It helped erase the painful memories of Japanese atrocities committed in Southeast Asian countries during World War II. The Belt and Road Initiative is not a Marshall Plan, nor is it similar to the Japanese program. But if China's foreign capital cooperation program also accounts for 5 per cent of its GDP, it will involve some US$500bn. It will take time for China to implement the project.

The Belt and Road initiative will involve interconnectivity via highways, railways, the power grid, the internet and an array of other infrastructure facilities, so that the equipment and products manufactured in China can be exported; and even more important, so that Chinese capital can be spent in global assistance programs. It should also be noted that, since 2015, China has officially become a 'net exporter of capital', with outbound investment overtaking inward foreign investment. Over time, China's ideas and soft power will be felt throughout the world.

'Made in China 2025' helps lay the foundation of a great financial era in China domestically, while the Belt and Road initiative helps create the external environment for a great financial era outside China. But I feel that I should use word 'greatest', rather than 'great', because never before in its 5,000-year-long civilization has China's influence been felt in every corner of the world, nor has its influence grown so dramatically. From my personal point of view, the arrival of the greatest era means the best of times, because China's 'internet plus' creates endless wealth. Over the past five years, China has created more than three times as many multimillionaires than Europe and the United States. Global wealth is concentrated in China. Of course, this also means bad times, because many of us are greedy and scared. The stock market crash this past month, which was both abrupt and inevitable, resulted in the elimination of 30,000 accounts that were worth Rmb5m, 250,000 accounts that were worth Rmb2m-5m. This can be attributed to the restlessness, bravado and fanaticism of the internet age. Last week, the CPC Central Committee issued *Guidelines on Promoting the Healthy Development of Internet Finance*, which defines the legal duties and responsibilities of the regulatory authorities. It also sets out regulatory boundaries and the bottom line of risk. A new era of rules- and standards-based supervision has been ushered into the sector, which effectively curbs the human greed for unruly growth of the industry, as well as the fear of uncertainty and other risk factors that may affect the industry.

I conclude by saying that we should embrace this great, internet-based financial era, but we must contain our greed and fear, the two most fundamental weaknesses of human nature. In this way, we will also embrace a great life in a great time.

THE GREATEST RISK OF REFORM IS THE FEAR OF RISK

It is essential for entrepreneurs to find opportunities. They are inherently risk-hungry, and in today's China, where pessimism prevails, it is much more important to secure opportunities than to avoid risks.

Unfortunately, people seem to pay more attention to risk than to opportunity. In my opinion, the decade prior to the 18th National Party Congress of the CPC was one when 'risk became the most feared', which is why risk is becoming almost a daily event. Fear of risk is, in fact, the greatest risk of the current reform. The more we fear risk, the less successful our reform will be.

Dr. Wang Wen made a keynote address at the Internet Finance and Personal Investment Risk Prevention Summit Forum in Wuhan on June 5, 2015.

I'D LIKE TO THANK THE ORGANIZERS FOR INVITING ME TO ADDRESS THIS forum on the topic of Internet Finance and Personal Investment Risk Prevention. In my opinion, it is quite an outdated topic even though it is also a quite hot one. They are at the same time relevant and out of touch with reality. Forgive me for saying this, for think tank scholars are well known for saying things that are not always pleasant to hear.

Why did I say it is both an outdated and hot topic?

I say it is a hot topic because over the past year or two, at least a thousand conferences on similar topics have been held in Beijing, Shanghai, Guangzhou and Shenzhen. While at Chongyang, it took our senior researcher, Mr. Huang Zhen, just a few weeks to create the 'Internet Finance Committee of 1000'. The first meeting we convened last year was packed with well over a thousand delegates. You can see how important this topic is, and it's just the right time to address it.

But why then outdated? To paraphrase a popular saying in Beijing's academic circle, 2013 was the first year of internet finance, while 2014 was the year of internet financial supervision. What about 2015? It looks as if the internet finance craze has become a thing of the past. The most popular socially operational model includes Alipay P2P, crowd-funding, or 'payment, finance, credit plus the internet', as well as the model known as 'all social functions plus the internet'. This is the concept of 'internet plus' as stipulated in the 2015 Government Work Report. Internet finance is just one of the new normal states of the 'internet plus' society. Besides, there are e-government, e-commerce, e-payment, online education, online travel, cloud computing, big data, network security, the internet of things, car networking, mobile medicine, cloud platform, and so on, many of which appeal to entrepreneurs.

Now, why then practical relevance and yet out of touch with reality? Because we have the honor of having many officials representing the government's financial supervisory body here today, and the topic pertains to their responsibility as policy makers who formulate policies that are meant to guard against risks. Besides, many scholars are also interested in topics that fall into this category. But on the other hand, we also have hundreds of business executives here today. In fact, entrepreneurs are more aware of risk prevention and risk aversion than scholars and officials.

I visited Alibaba on a research tour in 2014. I was impressed by what I heard from a senior executive. "Now, so many people are talking about the risks of internet finance, and worried about Alibaba's Alipay and Taobao," he said. "However, we actually worry more about risks than anyone else. If we do have a big risk, hundreds of millions of Taobao and Alipay users will subject Jack Ma to public denunciation."

For entrepreneurs, it is more important for them to find opportunities. Entrepreneurs themselves are the most risk-hungry, and in China, where pessimism prevails, it is much more important to secure opportunities than to avoid risks. Unfortunately, people seem to pay more attention to risk than to opportunity. The decade prior to the 18th National Party Congress of the CPC, I am afraid, was one when 'risk became the most feared', which is why risk is becoming an almost daily occurrence. For example, there have been very few bond market defaults over the past decade, and many project borrowers have never considered paying back their bank loan, because the government can write off their debts. Can this still be called a bond market? When the US financial crisis broke out in 2008, the Chinese government implemented a US$4tn stimulus policy fearing that China would be affected by the financial meltdown. The negative consequences of the stimulus policy are still felt today. So, fear of risk is in fact the greatest risk of the current reform.

The more a reform is designed to avoid risk, the less successful that reform will be. Ironically, the China Securities Regulatory Commission (CSRC) has made its contribution to this prevailing mentality by highlighting the risks inherent in the stock market and in finance generally.

In fact, a comparison across different industries would lead us to conclude that China is still abundant with opportunities and large development potential. China's current consumption contribution is about 50 per cent, but in developed countries it is 70 per cent; China's urbanization rate is roughly estimated to be about 50 per cent, but in developed countries it is about 80 per cent.

Think of the people who have gone abroad for fear of risk over the past decade or two: basically they all lost money. A popular joke goes like this: in 1999, someone sold his apartment within Beijing's Second Ring

Road. After toiling for 15 years in the US, he had earned US$1m. Yet the small apartment he sold is now worth Rmb7m. This is actually quite realistic.

At present, the non-performing loan ratio of Chinese banks is about 1.5 per cent, but towards the end of 1990s, it stood at about 20 per cent. China's local debt is about 40 per cent, compared with 100 per cent in some developed countries. Today, people seem to have far less tolerance of and preference for risk than in the past. Currently, as many as 94 per cent of Chinese households have investable assets of less than US$100,000, compared with below 50 per cent in a typical developed market. And this vast customer group is often faced with difficulties of financing channels and a lack of effective financial services. It is expected that, by 2020, the coverage rate of fund investment and wealth management in China will be raised from 3 per cent to 25-30 per cent, which is basically equal to that of developed markets; the coverage rate of small and micro financing in China will be raised from 11 per cent to 30-40 per cent, and financing channels will be provided to more than 30m small and micro enterprises and individual businesses that are not currently covered. From this perspective, it is not just internet finance we want to promote; the key is how to serve the people with 'inclusive finance', which will become a powerful boost of China's financial reform.

For internet finance, I think the biggest risk comes from moral hazard (knowingly violating the law, fraud), ignorance (don't know, don't understand, don't ask) and policy risk (changing all the time). Credit, market, law, operational and other risks are not significantly higher than the risks in traditional financial institutions. Moreover, the latter risk is controllable and can be reduced at an affordable level through certain measures. Finally, from the perspective of personal investment, how to deal with risk? I have two points to share with you. One is that the era of low risk, low threshold and high returns may be over. Investors must be realistic and must not think about making a fortune overnight. Second, the government, society and capital should combine forces. Chinese investors should regain their spirit of the market and rekindle the enthusiasm of being entrepreneurs.

In 1992, the market spirit was known as 'savage growth', literally meaning 'unregulated growth'. Now, it is normative growth, which means, 'doing what is permitted by law'. Respect the rules of the market, and there will be a return on your investment.

WHY ARE YOU SO PESSIMISTIC ABOUT CHINA'S ECONOMY?

The process of reform and opening up in the past 40 years is known as 'challenge emerging and then being addressed, and challenge re-emerging and then being addressed again'. Through a comprehensive understanding of the internal logic of pessimism and developing the theory of political economy with Chinese characteristics, we will be able to make sense of China's economic reality and its future trajectory. Meanwhile, we should reach consensus and build coherence, contribute our wisdom, minimize the impact of economic pessimism and ultimately boost the nation's confidence in the future of China's economy.

Between 2015 and 2016, China's economy suffered tremendous pressure resulting from the economic downturn. It seemed that pessimism had prevailed. Dr. Wang Wen was invited to attend several major forums and seminars at home and abroad. This article is based on the transcripts of one of his speeches.

IN RECENT YEARS, PUBLIC OPINION HAS TENDED TO BE VERY NEGATIVE ABOUT China's economic downturn, which resonates with the pessimism prevailing in other aspects of Chinese life. The negativity severely hurts investor confidence, thus presenting a potential, yet serious threat to political governance in China. In the long run, it will also affect the country's social stability and political unity. From this point of view, boosting confidence in the future of China's reform should become an important policy orientation, along with defusing destructive criticism from within China and overseas. This is just as important as macroeconomic policy control and deepening reform.

Theories that exaggerate the downward pressure on China's economy

Combing through the speculation about China's economy, some appear plausible. While citing classic Western economic theories, they actually sound too pessimistic; since the end of the 1990s, some have been alarmist, predicting that China will inevitably fall into chaos. Similar arguments can be divided into three categories:

First, a partial overview of short-term fluctuations of certain economic and financial sectors as the overall future of the Chinese economy. For example, after the huge volatility of the stock market in the summer of 2015, there have been many criticisms at home and abroad about the decline of China's financial sector, and even a warning of a crash in China's securities market. These arguments ignore the positive significance of last year's stock market volatility, which was to signal a major warning about the immaturity of China's securities market, its unsound financial system and the complexity of the international market. It is also a significant reversal of the structural characteristics of the securities market, which is dominated by retail and institutional investors that behave in a similar way to retailers. It is also an important experience in the progress of constructing multi-level capital markets with Chinese characteristics. Fundamentally, the idea that 'China will be in chaos and this will affect the world' has greatly underestimated China's ability to withstand slight fluctuations. It also ignores the comprehensive understanding of the long-term, difficult and tortuous nature of the so-called 'great historical struggle'. The process of comprehensively deepening reform is not only a revision of individual policies, but also a readjustment of the interests of all parties, the entire set of rules and the state structure, covering political, economic, social, military and diplomatic aspects. It is a very difficult process, and major adjustments must involve small fluctuations. But from a strategic point of view, we will find that some ups and downs may be temporary and short-lived. Of course, from a philosophical point of view, problems and contradictions are eternal; the key lies in how to solve the problems and contradictions in the process of development.

Second, regarding the inability of some people to adapt to the actual situation. For example, abandoning extensive growth, growth by emission, growth by selling land, growth by corruption and so on, has left some people confused and disorientated; the unregulated growth of high-grade, luxury, tobacco and alcohol sectors has been checked and balanced, leaving some sectors on the verge of depression; officials dare not seek wealth through power abuse, 'as long as nothing happens, they prefer not to do anything', resulting in a decline in work efficiency in some fields. Such mentality exists in many sectors, but they do not represent the whole of China. It is short-sighted to view the crackdown on past "acts of abnormal behavior" as downside risks of development. More often than not, this viewpoint represents a failure to see the gestation of new economic growth points, such as 'internet plus' and 'shared economy'. In fact, the contribution of consumption to economic expansion continues to grow, and a clean social interaction norm and ethics is being established and will continue to take on a benign, healthy trend. In addition, to make matters worse, critics ignore the improvement of social ethos and the recent macro perception of a better economic structure. In the past three or four years, a remolding of the national mentality has been accomplished. Most of the public have begun to adapt to these changes, and most officials have started to consciously resist corruption, the rules have been observed and green development has prevailed. Innovation is now the new normal, while entrepreneurship has become the mainstay. The country has significantly curbed the negativity that has worsened in many aspects of our social life.

The third is short-sightedness and arbitrariness. This argument views the short-term weakness of technological innovation as a permanent global growth dilemma. For example, some argue that China is now mired in a dotcom bubble that could spill over and impact the world's economic future. In fact, they ignore the dark and mediocre laws that have prevailed on the eve of the new technological revolution over the years. At present, various countries have introduced a large number of stimulus policies for technological innovation, such as 'Industrial 4.0' in Germany, 'The industrial internet' in the US, and 'Made in China 2025', which aims to integrate both traditional industries and the IT sector. China actually has a huge latecomer advantage in accelerating an intelligent, high-end and low-carbon economy in key industries. In many of its provinces, the actual value added of the core industries of the information economy has increased at an average annual rate higher than GDP growth, with the rapid development of new internet formats such as micro-commerce, e-commerce, the internet of things, cloud computing and big data, and has formed a unique competitive advantage for China's future development. Relying on the adhesive and catalyst function of the information and shared economies, China will promote the upgrading and transformation of traditional industries. By seeking a rebirth for its real economy, China will eventually seize the global opportunity in the new round of scientific and technological revolution and industrial transformation.

Three 'unchanged elements' are key to sustainable growth in China

Contrary to the pessimism that prevails in certain segments of society, the general public at large remains optimistic about the future of the country. Social factors that support the long-term stability and sound fundamentals of China's economy, from the general public to the government, from the international to the domestic, have not wavered. These factors are key to keeping China's economy growing at medium and high rates for a long time.

First, the upward mentality of the Chinese people has not changed. The 'getting rich through hard work' mentality that prevailed in the early days of reform and opening up has made outstanding entrepreneurs the role models of society, making hard work and success the mainstream of the Chinese zeitgeist. It has also become China's future growth engine. In light of the downward pressure of China's economy, a large number of enterprising self-employed workers, entrepreneurs and investors have set off a new wave of 'mass entrepreneurship', 'grassroots entrepreneurship' and 'grassroots economy'. In the first three quarters of 2016, there were 4.01m new registered enterprises nationwide, an increase of 27 per cent over the same in the previous year. Some 14,600 new enterprises were registered every day, which was significantly higher than the 12, 000 in 2015 and 10,000 in 2014. The tertiary industry accounts for 81.1 per cent of the total number of newly registered enterprises. Education, cultural, sports and entertainment industries, scientific research and technology services, information transmission software and information technology services enterprises are growing rapidly. All kinds of business incubators, agglomeration areas and service platforms flourish. New products, new technologies, new business patterns, new models continue to emerge. Crowdfunding, mass innovation, crowdsourcing and public service represent the brightest growth points. A new trend referred to by Premier Li Keqiang as "popular entrepreneurship and innovation" is in the making. In the 40 years since reform and opening up, the mentality of upward mobility and resilience prevailing among the Chinese public has remained the engine of China's future economic growth.

Second, the trend of China's economic transformation and upgrading has not changed. In 2015, China's urbanization rate reached 56.1 per cent, far below the average of about 80 per cent in developed countries in Europe and North America. The acceleration of urbanization in China will create new consumption and investment demand for economic growth. China has the largest total population and largest middle class population in the world. In the first three quarters of 2016, its total retail sales of social consumer goods increased by 10.4 per cent compared with the same period last year, and the contribution rate of consumption to national economic growth reached 71 per cent, much higher than the 66.4 per cent in 2015 and 51 per cent in 2014, making it the true stabilizer and ballast of economic growth. With the gradual implementation of supply side structural reform, smart consumption, energy saving, green consumption, service consumption, quality consumption, convenience consumption and safety consumption will continue to grow steadily, and the consumption structure will also continue to optimize. China is expected to become the world's largest manufacturer as well as the largest exporter, and is set to overtake the US as the world's largest consumer market in the years to come. This process will provide many business opportunities, not only in terms of creating a large market for investors around the world, but also providing momentum for the new round of economic growth in China. China's emerging industries are also growing rapidly, with huge potential for health, cultural services, energy conservation and environmental protection, and new energy, with an estimated cumulative output potential of Rmb60tn-80tn.

Third, the policy margin for China's reform and opening up has not changed. Reform and opening up is the biggest dividend of China's economic growth. Since the 18th CPC National Congress, the strategic determination to maintain reform and opening up and overcoming downward pressure has not wavered. Through further reform and opening up to generate vitality and promote long-term stable economic development, China's policy-makers have many tools at their disposal to cope with the economic slowdown, and they can take appropriate actions in due course. At present, China's debt ratio is far lower than that of major developed economies such as the US, the EU and Japan, and about 40 per cent of its debt is concentrated in infrastructure, social security and areas connected to people's livelihood. The higher national savings rate offers more room for investment and consumption, the reserve ratio and bank benchmark interest rate are higher, so there is enough room for fiscal and monetary policy to regulate liquidity. With the promotion of the Belt and Road initiative and the start-up of the AIIB and Silk Road Fund, cross-border cooperation in capacity and equipment manufacturing will be accelerated. These measures constantly help release the dividends of reform and opening up, stimulate the enthusiasm of enterprises and investors, and provide a new source of power for the next round of economic vitality and maintaining long-term and high-speed growth. Thanks to these consistent factors, China's economy will remain at the forefront of global growth for a long time. Between 2010 and 2015, the growth rate of the global economy was

5. 4 per cent, 4. 2 per cent, 3. 4 per cent, 3. 3 per cent, 3. 4 per cent and 3.1 per cent. China's contribution to global economic growth has been prominent for a long period of time, at 9.2 per cent, 10.6 per cent, 9.5 per cent, 7.7 per cent, 7.3 per cent and 6.9 per cent, equivalent to between twice and two-and-a-half times the average global growth rate. On three occasions, in April, June and October 2016, the International Monetary Fund (IMF) revised its forecast for global economic growth. While its economic growth estimates for the US, Europe and Japan were all frequently lowered, the forecast for China's economic growth actually rose, reflecting the confidence in China's future by a major international economic organization. Since 2016, many overseas media outlets have reported that China's economy is undergoing the 'growing pains' of transition, and that the economic slowdown is temporary and China's economic growth will remain strong in the future. A TIME magazine article claimed that 'China's decade' has begun, and the rise of China is unstoppable. China bashing has been eclipsed by the fact that the international community is optimistic about the Chinese economy. Despite the positive commentary, however, we still need to guard against complacency.

What is most needed now is policy assurance

Against the background of complex global public opinion, Chinese society needs to be able to distinguish between right and wrong, to discard the false and retain the true. China needs some 'noise'. Such noise, often in the form of worry and criticism, can be seen as a socially responsible response to China's development, or as anxiety about the country's uncertain future. However, it should not evolve into pride of some theoretical fundamentalism and prejudice against Chinese experimentalism. China's economic decision-makers and the mainstream of the society need resolve and endurance so that the success stories behind the economic reform and the public perception of the success story can dispel the impact of negative press at home and abroad. To that end, China's economic decision-makers need to do two things: reduce the frequency of short-term economic error; and allow some room for popular expectation of the long-term vision.

The process of reform and opening up in the past 40 years is in itself a process known as 'challenge emerging and challenge being addressed, and challenge re-emerging and challenge being addressed once again'. Through a comprehensive understanding of the internal logic of pessimism and developing the theory of political economy with Chinese characteristics, we will be able to gain a deeper understanding of China's economic reality and development trend. We should build consensus and coherence, contribute our wisdom, minimize the impact of pervasive economic pessimism and ultimately strengthen the nation's confidence in the future of China's economy.

DEVELOPING 'MADE WITH CHINESE INTELLECT' DOES NOT MEAN GIVING UP LABOR-INTENSIVE MANUFACTURING INDUSTRY

We want to say goodbye to the 'world factory' label because we are promoting what is known as *Made with Chinese Intellect*. However, this sloganeering may be rather optimistic and out of touch with the current reality in China. Don't forget the fact that 'Made in China' has contributed tremendously to China's economic expansion over the past 40 years, or even longer.

Sponsored by the Economic View of the New Media, China News Agency, The V Forum on Finance and Economics in China, 'China's Intellect and New Opportunities' was held in Beijing in 2017. This paper is based on the transcript of Dr. Wang Wen's speech.

I'D LIKE TO THANK THE ORGANIZERS FOR INVITING ME TO ADDRESS THIS great gathering on such a fine occasion. Before I arrived, I searched for the English equivalent for the Chinese word 'zhi', but to no avail. Some came up with 'Made by China', but that means 'created by China'; others went to great lengths to publish academic papers elaborating on the term, but once again it all ended up with poor translation.

In fact, *Made with Chinese Intellect* is not a phrase coined by professionals, but it means, according to public opinion in China, that we are rethinking about the future of Made in China at this historical conjuncture. By that I mean human society has progressed to the 'Era of Industry 4.0', from mechanization, electric power and information into an era of artificial intelligence. What is the future of 'Made with Chinese intellect'? It is such an important topic now that it has been discussed at both the annual National People's Congress and the Chinese People's Political Consultative Conference.

But I want to make myself clear that even if you are here to talk about Made with Chinese Intellect, we should not deny or forget the historic achievements that Made in China has accomplished. Neither should one imagine that China, a large manufacturing power, can afford to cease producing socks, clothes, food and other small commodities. This is simply not possible. Even if we talk about a future when we will innovate, create new brands and own intellectual property, it is still impossible to imagine that China, with a population of 1.4bn, will have to do away with labor-intensive industries. My first response to this viewpoint, which is very popular among the media, is that it may be too optimistic and too unrealistic if we want to stop to shut down this 'factory of the world'. That said, Made with Chinese Intellect is not intended to replace or completely deny what is Made in China, nor should we deny Made in China in the future. The truth is we must have a very clear understanding of our population, our national conditions and our complex social realities. Thus, no one should cherish any illusions about de-industrialization, because if that happens, our manufacturing industry will cease to exist.

Second, I argue that we should not forget Made in China because we must remain true to our original aspiration. That aspiration has to do with one thing, and one thing only: don't forget that Made in China has contributed tremendously to China's economic expansion over the past 30 or 40 years, or even more than half a century. Now there seems to be a public misperception that Made in China isn't working. It has produced little more than pollution and sweatshops. I don't think this is a fair criticism. So, on this occasion, I'd rather speak out in support for Made in China. Let us not forget that, over the past 40 years of reform and opening up, Made in China has helped us accomplish at least four important goals in which we take great pride. It is very important to know that, not only has it improved our livelihoods, but also the livelihoods of people from across the world. This is especially true for modern-day China, and it used to be known as self-sufficiency. What name do we give it now? We are rich and we enjoy the affluence very much. Many of you here are young. We have just observed the Chinese new year. In the past, one thing that delighted us during the spring festival was that we were given new clothes to wear as part of the new year celebrations. Alas, who here today still cherishes such an idea? None of you, I imagine, because we can wear new clothes every day. In the past, there was a supply shortage of just about everything, so we could only afford to wear new clothes during the festival seasons. This is by no means the case now. Since 2009, China has had more than 200 industrial sectors in which it ranks first in the world. According to statistics on small commodities published by a South Korean think tank, there were more than 1,400 commodities in the world in 2014. China's output was first in the world, followed by Germany. Germany was the leading producer of more than 400 items, and the United States more than 300. Therefore, Chinese consumers are actually the beneficiaries of the institutional dividend as well as the national economic development dividend. In sum, we owe our improved living standards to Made in China.

The second one is also very important in my opinion. Through Made in China, we gradually built up an entire industrial chain. We can roll out almost all small items. About five years ago, an Israeli told me a story. When smartphones first appeared, an Israeli showed off his selfie in a video. He used a pole to hold up that phone, saying it would change our future lives. To make it a reality, he wanted to raise money to mass produce the pole. However, two months later, Chinese selfie sticks began to sell like hot cakes. That shows China's ability to mimic and manufacture. The Chinese can come back with a replica simply at a glance of the original, which is the world's leading replicative power associated with Made in China. Of course, the ability to replicate is also controversial.

Third, I think that the most important thing about Made in China is that it has changed the global economic landscape. Since World War II, 120 newly independent countries have emerged, yet for more than half a century none has advanced from low-income to high-income. That said, China can be the best candidate to become a high-income country. China has now become a middle-to-high income country, and in a few years it will certainly become a high-income one. Once again, Made in China has changed the world's economic landscape. I feel that Made in China deserves the credit.

Last but not least, Made in China creates a riddle for the international intellectual community. Until now, that mystery has remained unresolved by international scholars and experts involved in the study of social sciences. The mystery is why China has risen. In fact, many scholars, in China and overseas, try to explain why China has been transformed over the past 40 years, with no change in system and still the same people. Many scholars have tried their best to explain this miracle in terms of economic development. Some of them came up with their own answers, but I'm afraid they have yet to agree on a single answer.

My third point of view to share with you is the notion of Made with Chinese Intellect. I find it a new source of energy even though I think highly of the previous notion known as Made in China. Yet, there was strong backlash against Made in China from a small minority of public intellectuals and academics, who complained about the moral defects of Made in China, such as high levels of pollution, poor working conditions, exploitation of the working class and a lack of dignity afforded those working on assembly lines. Of course, these are reasonable complaints. However, the desire and motivation of entrepreneurs are not subject to moral judgment. More important, economists worldwide have long abandoned the use of moral variants.

What connects Made in China with Made with Chinese Intellect is a common desire to pursue profit. The key is that we want those business owners to see where their rights and interests lie and where the benefits lie. If we can identify such a point of interest, the transformation will become easier. Where is the converging point of interest?

Now that the world's economic landscape is changing, I find a group of statistics very enlightening. Over the past 20 years or so, China's exports have accounted for a rising share of domestic growth and international economic growth, and there is a growing interdependence between the two. China's exports are rising every year, but the growth in the production of all commodities in the country is declining year by year. In the middle of the 1990s, almost all Made in China products accounted for 80 per cent of our domestic growth. What is meant by that? Simply put, a considerable amount of what we call growth is exported, amounting to 80-90 per cent. But now the export rate has dropped to 40-50 per cent, chiefly because most of the commodities are now for domestic consumption.

The second is that the increase in output of products for foreign markets has increased year by year, at a level of about 10 per cent in the mid-1990s. Our production output now accounts for about 50 per cent of the world's total. What does this interlacing tell us? First, Made in China is already 'Made for the World'. Indeed, Chinese manufacturing is all about making things for world consumption. From this point of view, the world owes China a word of thanks since we often end up polluting our environment in order to produce for the world.

Second, it's important to note that China's domestic market is getting bigger; in 2015 alone, our annual domestic consumption reached Rmb30tn. In three to five years or so, China's consumer market will become the largest in the world. The Chinese consumers' rising demand should translate into the most powerful incentive for entrepreneurs. If we don't shift to Made with Chinese intellect, Chinese consumers will have to continue buying smart toilets from Japan. For an entrepreneur, that is a big loss of profit.

Similarly, where is the largest potential increase in export trade? My answer is, in the 'Belt and Road' areas that we have been talking about. The growth in this region is so high. Over the past six years or so, world trade has grown at a lower rate than world GDP, that is to say, less than 3 per cent. However, China's international trade growth, together with the regional trade expansion in Belt and Road countries, has averaged at 20-30 per cent over the past three years or so. The growth rate reached as high as 40-50 per cent in some countries in that region. Indeed, the Belt and Road project areas present enormous opportunities to both Made in China and Made with Chinese Intellect.

When we talk about Made with Chinese Intellect today, there are three things to be noted for the future. These are also mentioned in my 'Made in China 2025', and I will repeat them here.

First, I think the amount of R&D will continue to increase in the next five years and, more important, we need to promote the deep integration of information technology and industrialization in China. At present, we face a very big opportunity in industries such as the new generation IT sector, high-end CNC machine tools and robotics, aerospace, power equipment, agricultural machinery, new materials and biomedical industries. It is in these areas where we are facing the task of upgrading the Made in China technologies. The successful upgrading of China's technologies will present a major opportunity for China to lead the world.

Second, Chinese companies need to enhance their international and domestic marketing awareness. This is long overdue. In fact, while many Chinese companies are doing well, our brand value has not been increased.

One last point: we need to fully implement green manufacturing. In the next five to ten years, China's carbon emissions will be greatly reduced, but only if we are committed to going green.

There are unprecedented opportunities for products made in China or made with Chinese intellect. Of course, there are challenges, but challenge also means opportunity and that promises profits. Thank you.

ENHANCING OCEAN AWARENESS AND SOLVING CHINA'S ECONOMIC PREDICAMENT

We should vigorously enhance the awareness of ocean development through various means and channels, and publicize the strategic importance of the ocean in China's nation building and economic development process so that we can raise public awareness of oceans as territory and part of our national economy, and manage the oceans through the rule of law. We should educate the general public and create the most favorable conditions conducive to caring for, developing and protecting the ocean.

September 26, 2016, The China-Qingdao International Summit Forum on the Development of Ocean was held in Qingdao, China. Dr. Wang Wen delivered a keynote address at the forum. This paper is a condensed version of the speech, published in the 2016 No. 19 issue of China Finance.

WITH THE STRATEGIC PLAN OF 'BUILDING CHINA AS A SEA POWER' AND THE promotion of the Belt and Road initiative strategy put forward by the 18th National Congress of the CPC, ocean development has been elevated to the level of national strategy. Building China into a powerful marine nation is of great significance for promoting sustained and healthy economic development, and safeguarding national sovereignty, security and economic interests. The July 12, 2016 South China Sea Arbitration Case was a wake-up call and a reminder of the urgency of building China into a maritime power.

However, at present, China still lags behind in terms of its capacity for marine development, the utilization of marine resources is still in its infancy and the proportion of the marine industry in GDP is far lower than that in developed countries. In particular, the development of marine finance based on the concept of the 'ocean belonging to the people' is still falling behind, which seriously hinders the development and utilization of the ocean. According to the State Oceanic Administration, the country's marine GDP totaled Rmb6.46tn in 2015, accounting for 9.6 per cent of total GDP, and is expected to reach 15 per cent by 2030. Currently, the marine economy of developed countries accounts for more than 20 per cent of GDP, and the coastal and marine economies of the US account for 51 per cent of both GDP and employment. The absolute value is 10 times greater than that in our country. At a time when China's land resources cannot bear the pressure of further sustained development, financial means have been used to integrate resources and channels to encourage the public to participate in and benefit from the development and utilization of the ocean. Thus, the concept of 'investing in the ocean and benefiting from the ocean' has become the key to solving the issue of ocean development in China, to cultivating a new economic growth point and breaking the predicament of China's future development.

The development of marine finance faces many constraints

At present, financial services for the development of the marine industry in our country are quite limited, especially given the traditional core focus on developing the land-based economy. Therefore, China's development of marine finance still faces many challenges.

First, the institutional and policy framework and the lack of experience on the part of financial institutions restrict the development of marine finance. China still lacks an integrated strategy for marine development, without a systematic policy framework or directives as guidance, and most of China's development models are labor-intensive. In addition, China's marine economy is still in its infancy, many companies are small in size and scale, so we must have a sense of urgency to implement the overall plan to develop the marine economy. Due to a lack of scientific guidance and financial support, the average development rate of marine biological resources around China is less than 20 per cent, and the processing rate of aquatic products is only 30 per cent. The exploitation and utilization of chemical and energy resources are more backward, and the development and utilization of the more than 150 coastal tourist projects are in the primary stage. Most of the loans issued by banks are secured and pledged. However, the right to use the sea area and the right to profit are restricted by many policies and regulations, and mortgage financing is greatly restricted. It is much more difficult for marine businesses to reach the expected financing scale than for land-based enterprises. At the same time, compared with the land-based economy, the marine industry has fewer tools at its disposal to boost its assets. In other words, the traditional financing mode runs short of new financing and risk management tools to satisfy the needs of a modern marine industry. Many enterprises that undertake projects, especially private enterprises, do not have sufficient fixed assets, while the operating costs (including business assessment and risk management) for offshore financial operations are higher. As a result, banks and other financial institutions have long tended to devote their limited energy to the R&D and marketing of terrestrial financial products, where policies and processes are relatively mature. Deliberately or unintentionally, they avoid getting involved in the sea.

Second, the marine industry, which faces great potential risks, is not attractive to financial institutions. Frequent marine disasters and export-oriented enterprises' exchange rate risk are practical problems that must be addressed in the development of the marine economy. In the absence of a targeted risk mitigation mechanism, banks face greater risks in financing marine enterprises. More important, in the case of maritime rights and disputes with sovereign countries, the development of the marine industry may also face geopolitical risks arising from maritime rights disputes. In the East and South China Seas, tensions tend to run high due to provocative behavior by regional and extra-territorial nations. Regional tensions add to the uncertainty, which is a risk factor that financial services institutions have to consider when servicing the marine economy.

Third, the lack of specialized marine financial institutions. The development of the marine economy requires many specialized financial institutions to provide customized financial services. In order to best serve the marine economy, financial service providers should be integrated and adapted to the development of the marine economy. China has yet to establish a comprehensive financial institution dedicated to the marine economy. Only a few banks offer some basic services, so they cannot fully integrate their various resources and channels, or their investment, financing, insurance or other business platforms. It is difficult to carry out broader, maritime-related business activities.

Fourth, Chinese society needs to enhance its awareness of the country's oceanic interests. The fact that society lacks this awareness has resulted in the backwardness of the marine industry and marine science and technology, making China quite overstretched in areas such as ocean problem-solving and having an open policy toward ocean exploration, with new and old problems intertwining. It has jeopardized national sovereignty, territorial integrity and relations with our neighboring countries.

Multiple measures should be taken to strengthen marine finance

First, government policy and institutional support is a prerequisite. The government needs to strengthen policy- and institution-building, provide financial institutions with financial security through policy guidance and various monetary policy instruments, and encourage financial institutions to optimize their credit structures, so as to guide the agglomeration of financial resources into the marine economy. It is suggested that special funds may be allocated from government resources, with social capital involved, to establish a government-dominated fund of mixed ownership that is devoted solely to the development of the marine industry. The government can use this fund to grant financial subsidies and tax relief to infrastructure, public services and industrialization and other projects. We can also establish a comprehensive trading platform for property rights, marine science and a financial alliance for marine science and technology and so on. Take Singapore as an example. The Singapore government has been praised for its efforts to develop the marine economy and marine finance: the establishment of a special industrial zone administration, and the promulgation of policies such as the *Emerging Industries Act* and the *Economic Expansion Award Act* to encourage related industries; a maritime finance incentive plan, with which the government guides social capital to enter the marine industry through tax benefits, hence the establishment of the Singapore maritime transportation trust fund.

It is necessary to strengthen the organization building of local banking regulatory bodies, establish an intra-governmental communication and cooperation mechanism between local banking regulatory bodies, the local National Development and Reform Commission, the Environmental Protection Bureau and other departments, so that these national organizations can provide consultation services for the industrial planning of local governments. It is also necessary to work with local governments to carry out special research projects, such as building a 'government-bank enterprise' information-sharing platform and key projects docking platform. Meanwhile, we should actively broaden financing channels, use multi-level capital markets to raise funds for the development of the marine economy and increase the liquidity of marine assets.

In order to build a sustainable financial support system for the marine sector, we should enhance the ability of the marine economy to absorb financial capital through financial policies that allow multiple entities to participate at various levels and which optimize the investment and financing environment. This is not only the basic condition for the integration of financial and industrial capital in the development of the marine economy, but also a necessary condition for effective regional planning and strategic management of the marine economy. Second, it is necessary to improve the capacity of marine resources development and facilitate the transformation of the marine economy to one of quality, efficiency and high innovation. By improving capacity and expanding the field of marine development, the marine economy will become a new growth point for our economy. We must also accelerate the upgrading of marine fisheries, shipbuilding, chemicals and other industries, agglomerate and develop the port sector, and build the industrial system and industrial clusters with complete chains, armed with advanced technology and with distinctive characteristics. We should also endeavor to strengthen the planning and guidance of the marine economy, improve the quality of marine economic growth, and optimize and expand the marine industry.

Besides, it is a fact that the growth of China's marine economy has long been driven mainly by resources, capital and labor input. Technological innovation has contributed only 30 per cent of the marine economy, compared with more than 70 per cent in developed countries. Therefore, we should strengthen marine science and technology R&D through innovation, promote the commercialization of the results of scientific and technological innovation, and improve the contribution rate of science and technology to the marine economy and international competitiveness.

Third, we should give full play to the role of financial institutions, speed up the innovation of financial hedging tools, and improve the mechanism of risk prevention and management in the marine economy. Banks are at the core of China's domestic financial system, so the system can fully integrate all kinds of resources and channels and make comprehensive use of investment, funds, financial leasing, insurance, trust firms, overseas institutions and other business platforms. Its purpose is to provide comprehensive credit, trade finance, financial consultation, draft business, agency bond issuance, investment banking, financial leasing, trust, financial advice for infrastructure construction and marine economy industrial chains, and financial services solutions of all types, such as marine insurance. Foreign trade enterprises are encouraged to hedge exchange rate risks through exchange rate futures, currency swaps and other products. Take, for instance, the financing businesses of Hong Kong and Singapore, which are relatively developed in marine finance. Unlike the bond financing model in the West, both these places use stocks and trust funds as the main financing channels, which is faster and cheaper than traditional bond financing. The rates of return are also higher. Not only can this contribute more effectively to the development of the marine economy, but also fully tap into the huge potential for business expansion intrinsically associated with the marine economy. Strengthening the risk-resisting ability of companies involved in the marine business will also help financial institutions innovate their own businesses and open up new channels for further development.

Meanwhile, it is high time to establish a maritime cooperative development bank. The establishment of such a bank will meet current demands and satisfy the inherent needs of China's sustainable economic development. It will speed up the transformation and upgrading of marine economic development and accelerate the construction of a powerful maritime nation. With the basic function of implementing national marine industry policy and promoting the coordinated development of the marine economy, a marine cooperative development bank, by supporting the infrastructure development of the marine industry, will guide the flow of social funds, and provide technology, management and talent, and information services to promote the growth and optimization of the marine industry. The bank may also serve to support the building of key national marine development zones and bring about the technological transformation and innovation projects of key marine sectors, adjust the imbalance and improve the investment layout of the marine investment structure, and further improve the overall function of the financial mechanism and enhance its regulatory role. Lastly, it will optimize the overall function of China's financial system in the development of the marine industry.

Fourth, think tanks will provide talent and intelligence support for the development of marine finance. The marine economy requires the best technology and expertise, so a lack of trained experts and professional personnel is an important factor hindering the development of marine finance. We need to set out from the strategic perspective of continuing to promote marine finance, vigorously develop marine science and technology, and support the training of marine talent, as well as promote 'mass entrepreneurship and innovation' in the field of the marine economy. Emphasis will be placed on training professionals who will be at the forefront of marine science and have international influence, expand the scale of marine education, strengthen discipline building and train high-level professionals. At the same time, it is also necessary to employ think tanks, academic institutions and practicing experts to provide services such as consulting on the development planning of marine financial services and major project reviews. With these experts, we can advise on the development of marine financing and provide intellectual support for the continued expansion of the marine finance sector.

Finally, we should attach great importance to the role of the private sector. Private capital is also a force that cannot be ignored in the marine economy. In addition to involving financial institutions and supporting the development of marine cooperation, private capital should be encouraged and channeled into the development of the marine industry and develop a diversified investment and financing mechanism. Third-party service organizations should be fully utilized to provide professional protection for the development of the marine financial industry. For instance, we should cooperate with shipping brokerage companies, professional insurance companies, law firms, professional independent inspection firms and other third-party service organizations. With the help of professional institutions, we can quickly obtain relevant information on marine enterprises and enhance the comprehensive service capacity of marine finance. Market participants should be encouraged to carry out marine financial innovation, optimize the environment of marine finance, raise the benchmark of the financial industry, and promote mutual assistance and interdependence between government and civil society.

More important, we should vigorously enhance the awareness of ocean development through various means and channels, and publicize the strategic position of the ocean in China's nation building and economic development process so that we can fundamentally raise public awareness of the oceans as territory and as part of the national economy, and manage the ocean through rule of law. We should educate the general public and create the most favorable conditions conducive to caring about the ocean, developing the ocean and protecting the ocean.

This paper was co-authored by Mr. Zhan Teng

ACKNOWLEDGMENTS

This book is the brainchild of a think-tank scholar who is fascinated by a China on the rise and looking forward to sharing with the world its success stories. It took an immense amount of time and work, and it would not exist without the invaluable contributions of a number of incredibly thoughtful and supportive people, who include:

Li Bing, Copyright Editor of People's Publishing House, who represented and supported me from inception to publication;

Cao Chun, Senior Editor of People's Publishing House , who offered encouragement, friendship and silence at all the right times;

Ying Mathieson, the ever-patient publisher of ACA Publishing Ltd, who helped bring this book to fruition;

David Lammie, Senior Editor of ACA Publishing, who offered editorial help and keen insight. He was important to getting this book published;

Finally, although my name is on the cover of this book, Teng Jimeng did most of the translation and deserves huge credit. Without him, the English version of this book would not exist.

Wang Wen

ABOUT THE AUTHOR

Dr. Wang Wen is a professor and the executive dean of Chongyang Institute for Financial Studies, Renmin University of China. He has visited nearly a hundred countries (as well as the South Pole), conducted extensive research and field investigations, and met with presidents and prime ministers in more than thirty countries.

Dr. Wang Wen is an influential think-tank scholar in China, specializing in global governance, major power relations, green finance and macroeconomic policies. His reports have been approved by Chinese policymakers on dozens of occasions. He has edited and written more than 30 books, several of which have become bestsellers.